PACIFIC REEF & SHORE

A PHOTO GUIDE TO NORTHWEST MARINE LIFE

RICK M. HARBO

HARBOUR PUBLISHING

Published by
Harbour Publishing Co. Ltd., P.O. Box 219, Madeira Park, BC V0N 2H0
www.harbourpublishing.com

Edited by Mary Schendlinger
Cover and page design and layout by Martin Nichols

Printed and Bound in Canada

This book is dedicated to my family: Heather, Jennifer, Michael and Amy, and to my many friends who provided their assistance and shared their love and knowledge of the sea.

Acknowledgements
Scientific editing and advice were generously provided by numerous experts in the development of this guide. My thanks to Ronald L. Shimek, William C, Austin, Claudia Mills, Daphne Fautin, Paul V. Scott, Eugene V. Coan, James McLean, Roger N. Clark, Sandra Millen, Neil McDaniel, Roland Anderson, Gregory Jensen, William Merilees, Philip Lambert, Gretchen Lambert, Charles Lambert, Andy Lamb, Graham Gillespie, Graeme Ellis, John Ford, Jane Watson, Jim Borrowman, Michael Hawkes, Sandra Lindstrom, Steve Dennis and Duane Sept.

Special thanks to the editor, Mary Schendlinger, for giving clarity to the descriptions and preparing the index. Howard White and Vici Johnstone provided valuable direction in the development of this guide. Mary White scanned photographs. Martin Nichols, Lionheart Graphics, contributed his talents to the design and layout of the book and the map on page 4.

Cover photographs and all other photos are copyright Rick M. Harbo, with the exception of spiny dogfish, six gill shark (p. 10), copyright Neil McDaniel; red octopus (p. 25), copyright Roland Anderson, Seattle Aquarium; and Spanish shawl (p. 24), copyright Duane Sept.

Illustrations (6) of marine mammals (pp. 7–8) were prepared by Pieter Folkens: harbour porpoise, Dall's porpoise, Pacific white-sided dolphin, orca, gray whale and humpback whale.

Harbour Publishing acknowledges the financial support of the Government of Canada through the Book Publishing Industry Development Program (BPIDP) and the Canada Council for the Arts, and the Province of British Columbia through the British Columbia Arts Council, for its publishing activities.

THE CANADA COUNCIL | LE CONSEIL DES ARTS
FOR THE ARTS | DU CANADA
SINCE 1957 | DEPUIS 1957

National Library of Canada Cataloguing in Publication Data
Harbo, Rick M., 1949–
    Pacific reef and shore : a photo guide to Northwest marine life /
Rick M. Harbo.

    Includes index.
    ISBN 1-55017-304-9

    1. Seashore biology—Pacific Coast (B.C.)—Identification.
2. Seashore biology—Pacific Coast (U.S.)—Identification. I. Title.
QH95.3.H38 2003   578.769'9'09795   C2002-911549-3

Contents

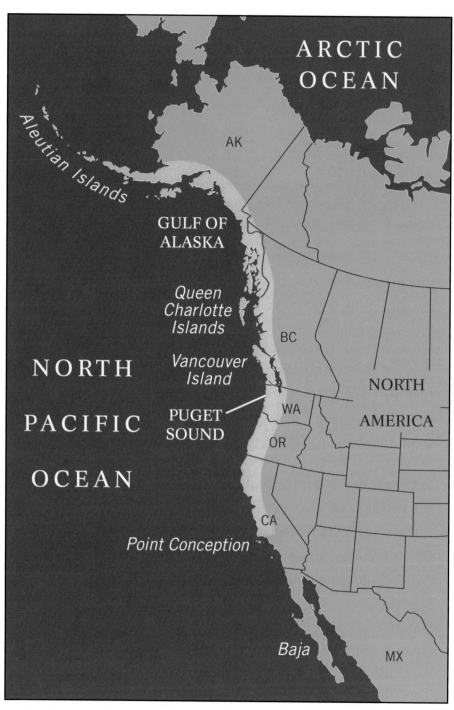

Northeast Pacific Ocean and the Pacific Northwest coast; the reefs and shores from the Aleutian Islands, Alaska to Point Conception, California.

Introduction

Thousands of fascinating creatures inhabit the beaches, tidepools and waves of the Pacific Northwest, and more than 300 species of marine animals and plants listed in this field guide are just those most commonly seen along the coast of Alaska, British Columbia, Washington, Oregon and northern California. Wonderful surprises await anyone—from the first-time beachcomber to the seasoned scuba diver—who spends an afternoon looking closely at the wildlife of our marine shores and waters.

Tides and Currents

Whether you are boating, diving or just walking along the seashore, you must be aware of the tides and currents in the area you are exploring. The earth's waters rise and recede, drawn by the gravitational pull of the moon, and to a lesser extent the sun. Tidal changes can be extreme, with a daily range in water height or depth of as much as 20' (6 m) in some locations. Tidal changes also cause swift currents at narrows where water flow is constricted. Tide and current tables, published by government agencies, are available at marinas and sporting goods stores, and local tide tables appear daily in most newspapers.

The best time to view marine life is during the two hours before and after the lowest tide, generally less than 2' (60 cm) in the USA and less than 3' (1 m) in Canada. If you are an experienced diver and you plan to visit current-swept areas for the rich marine life, plan your dives for slack times, as the tides change direction.

The **intertidal** area of the beach is the part that is submerged at high tide and exposed at low tide, a habitat where many animals and plants are covered and uncovered by water twice a day. Creatures that live here are adapted to the **high, mid-** and/or **low intertidal** zones. The subtidal area is the shallow water, that part of the salt water that is within diving range (less than 100'/30 m deep). Species here are always submerged, and they live in conditions of much less rugged surf and exposure to weather than intertidal dwellers.

Names of Species

Almost every plant and animal has a common name, usually local and often colourful, such as the northwest ugly clam. The scientific name (*Entodesma navicula* for the northwest ugly clam), a unique name composed of two words and registered with an international organization, gives scientists a standard, precise way of communicating information about a particular organism.

Scientific classifications and names are constantly under review as more is learned about wildlife, and species names change frequently, so there are often many names for a given plant or animal.

Marine Conservation

This guidebook is intended to help you identify animals and plants in their habitat without having to collect or otherwise disturb them. That is the best way to understand the relationships between organisms and their environment, and to protect them for future generations to observe and enjoy.

If you must take specimens, be aware of local Fisheries regulations and licensing requirements. Wherever possible, collect organisms from man-made structures such as docks and pilings. Take as few specimens as possible and avoid individuals that are laying or guarding eggs, or engaged in reproductive behaviours. If you dig into sand or mud, or turn over rocks, replace the disturbed material carefully and immediately. Avoid stepping on plants and animals.

There are many threats to the marine environment, including overfishing, pollution and habitat destruction. Many local or international marine conservation groups are active, and they will be glad to provide you with more information on enjoying and caring for the natural wonders of the coastline.

Marine Mammals

Whales, Dolphins, Porpoises, Seals & Sea Lions, Sea Otter & River Otter

Phylum Chordata

Illustrations by Pieter Folkens

Whales, Dolphins, Porpoises

▾ HARBOUR PORPOISE

Phocoena phocoena
To 6'3" (1.8 m) long. Weight to 145 lb. (65 kg). Low, triangular dorsal fin. Small rounded head. Dark back, light sides to white, speckled belly. Solitary or in pairs, in coastal areas year-round. Avoids vessels; does not bow-ride.

▲ PACIFIC WHITE-SIDED DOLPHIN

Lagenorhynchus obliquedens
To 8' (2.4 m) long. Weight to 300 lb. (135 kg). Tall, curved dorsal fin, black and grey. Black back with pale grey streak along sides, widening at tail end. Most abundant dolphin in north Pacific. Fast swimmer, leaps and creates "rooster tail" splash. In groups of 50 to several hundred.

DALL'S PORPOISE ▸

Phocoenoides dalli
To 7'3" (2.2 m) long. Weight to 485 lb. (218 kg). Hooked, triangular dorsal fin, often with white patch. Thick body, grey to black with white patch on sides and belly. Common and abundant. Fast swimmer; creates "rooster tail" splash. Often bow-rides.

◀ ORCA (Killer Whale)
Orcinus orca

Female to 23' (7 m), 4.5 tons (4 tonnes), short curved dorsal fin to 3' (90 cm). Male larger, to 30' (9 m) and 6 tons (5.4 tonnes), tall dorsal fin to 6' (1.8 m). Black with white chin, white patches behind eye and on sides. Dorsal fins and distinctive saddle patches behind dorsal fin used for identification. Family groups have unique vocalizations. Nearshore pods (5–50 animals) of resident orcas feed only on fish. Small pods (2–10 animals) of transient orcas are mammal hunters. Offshore orcas (pods to 25 or more animals) are likely fish eaters.

GRAY WHALE *Eschrichtius robustus* ▶

To 50' (15 m) long. Weight to 35 tons (31.5 tonnes). Long, slender head. A baleen whale (feeds by straining food through baleen plates in the jaws). Upper jaw has coarse yellow baleen. Grey body with lighter patches and mottling, scattered patches of white barnacles and orange whale lice. Low dorsal "hump," followed by 6 to 12 "knuckles." Marks on body sides and tail flukes are used to identify individuals. In shallow coastal waters; whales breed in shallow lagoons of Baja and migrate annually to Arctic seas.

HUMPBACK WHALE ▶
Megaptera novaengliae

To 49'3"(14.8 m) long. Weight to 44 tons (40 tonnes). Large head with small knobs. A baleen whale. Low, stubby dorsal fin with broad base. Long, slender flippers. Grey to black body with lighter underside. Alone or in groups of 20 or more. Swims actively, breaching, spyhopping and rolling on back to wave flippers. Many feeding behaviours, lunging and bubble-netting. Colour and shape of underside of tail flukes are used to identify individuals.

Seals, Sea Lions

▲ PACIFIC HARBOUR SEAL *Phoca vitulina richardsi*
Male and female to 6' (1.8 m) long. Weight to 250 lb. (113 kg). Large, round, smooth head without external ear flaps. Short, furry front flippers. Grey to black, mottled. Often hauls out on rocks and sand or mudflats.

▼ STELLER SEA LION
Eumetopias jubatus
Female to 8' (2.4 m), 600 lb. (270 kg); male to 10' (3 m), 2,200 lb. (990 kg). Ear flaps; low forehead. Large front flippers to sit erect. Male tan above and reddish brown below; female slimmer and uniformly brown. Roars and growls, does not bark. Hauls out on rocks.

▼ CALIFORNIA SEA LION
Zalophus californianus
Female to 5'8" (1.7 m), 250 lb. (113 kg); male to 8' (2.4 m) and 900 lb. (405 kg). Ear flaps. Smaller and darker than Steller sea lion. Mature male dark brown to tan, light-coloured bump on forehead. Female blonde to tan. Barks. Hauls out on rocks, logs and docks. Only males (below) migrate north of California.

(L) male, (R) female.

Males.

Sea Otter, River Otter

▲ SEA OTTER *Enhydra lutris*
To 5' (1.5 m) long. Weight to 80 lb. (36 kg). Short, flattened tail. Short, thick neck and flat, broad head. Large, webbed hind feet. Tan or rusty red to dark brown or black, with light-coloured head. Squeals, hisses and grunts. Uses rock as a tool while eating and floating belly-up. Often swims on its back. In open, exposed waters, solitary or "rafts" in kelp beds. Clumsy on land, seldom leaves the water.

▲ RIVER OTTER
Lutra canadiensis
To 4'6" (1.4 m) long. Weight to 30 lb. (13.5 kg). Long, round, tapered tail. Slender body and long neck, small, webbed hind feet. Short, dense dark fur above, lighter below. Unique whistle. Often swims belly-down. At home on land.

Fishes
Phylum Chordata

Sharks, Rays, Skates
These animals have cartilaginous skeletons.

▼ SPINY DOGFISH
Squalus acanthias
To 5'3" (1.6 m) long. Weight to 20 lb. (9 kg). Long, slender shark. Slate grey to brown with grey-white underside. A single spine at the front of each of the top (dorsal) fins. Small mouth. Bears live young, rather than eggs. At surface to 2,400' (720 m).

▼ SIX GILL SHARK
Hexanchus griseus
To 26'5" (8.8 m) long. Large head, 6 gill slits and a single dorsal fin. Dark brown to slate-grey with pale under-side. Known as a "cow shark," not known to be aggressive toward divers. Usually in deep waters, has been seen regularly at 30-100' (9-33 m).

◀ **RATFISH** *Hydrolagus colliei*
To 39" (1 m) long. Large snout, small mouth with forward-pointing teeth. Long, tapering tail. Grey-brown body **(A)** with white spots and silver underside. Swims by flapping forward fins. Male has large claspers on underside. Female lays eggs **(B)** in elongated cases. Often in shallows, 30–3,085' (9–925 m) deep.

Bony Fishes

These fishes have bony "spines" and a variety of body shapes. Many are the familiar species seen in tidepools and on reefs.

▼ **BIG SKATE** *Raja binoculata*
To 8' (2.4 m) long overall. Weight 200 lb. (90 kg)+. Pointed, V-shaped snout. Large eye-like spots near centre of each pectoral fin. Brown to dark grey. Rests on bottom, often partially buried, 10–2,625' (3–788 m) deep.

▼ **TIDEPOOL SCULPIN**
Oligocottus maculosus
To 3¹/₂" (9 cm) long. Slender body, single forked spine on gill cover. Colour varies, often red-brown to green; 5 irregular dark saddles across the back. Common only in tidepools.

▼ **SKATE EGG CASES**
(Mermaid's Purse)
Egg case of each species has a unique shape. Case of the big skate, *Raja binoculata*, may be up to 12" (30 cm) long and contain as many as 7 eggs. Often washed up on shore.

**SCALEYHEAD
SCULPIN**
Artedius harringtoni ▶
To 4" (10 cm) long. 2 pairs of bush appendages on head of male. Colour varies from red to brown; white spot at base of caudal fin. At 16–35' (5–10.5 m) deep.

LONGFIN SCULPIN ▶

Jordania zonope
To 6" (15 cm) long. Slender, tapered body. Colourful olive green, red-orange and blue bands. Distinctive pale bands on head. At 6–60' (2 –15 m) deep.

▼ SAILFIN SCULPIN

Nautichthys oculofasciatus
To 8" (20 cm) long. Pink-orange to brown with bands on the back. Unique tall, sail-like first dorsal fin. In crevices, on pilings in shallow subtidal to 360' (108 m) deep.

▲ RED IRISH LORD

Hemilepidotus hemilepidotus
To 20" (50 cm) long. Large head and eyes, conspicuous band of scales, 4 to 5 wide, along sides. Colourful yet camouflaged, with red patches and brown, black and white mottling. In rocky areas, usually motionless, intertidal to 162' (49 m) deep.

▼ BUFFALO SCULPIN

Enophrys bison
To 14$^{1/2}$" (36 cm) long. Large head with pair of prominent spines on gill cover. Raised plates along high lateral line. Colour varies from brown to pink and green, with 4 dark saddles across the back. Pink egg mass. On rocky reefs, 3–60' (1–15 m) deep.

▼ CABEZON

Scorpaenichthys marmoratus
To 39" (1 m) long. Weight to 30 lb. (13.5 kg). Large head, tapered body. Bushy, flap-like appendage on snout and above each eye. Marbled olive green to brown or grey, well camouflaged. On rocky reefs, in kelp, intertidal to 250' (75 m) deep.

◄ GRUNT SCULPIN
Rhamphocottus richardsoni
To 3¹/4" (8 cm) long. Unique
short, stout body with pointed
snout and small eye. Tan to
orange with dark bands.
"Hops" along the bottom. In
empty barnacle shells, in
sponges or rocky crevices,
6–540' (2–165 m) deep.

Rockfishes

Many of these common and popular commercial and sport fishes are long-lived,
but reef populations are easily overfished.

QUILLBACK ROCKFISH ►
Sebastes maliger
To 2' (60 cm) long. Dark brown to
black, mottled with yellow and orange.
High, spiny dorsal fin with yellow
streak in forward region. On rocky
reefs, surface to 480' (144 m) deep.

▼ YELLOWEYE ROCKFISH
Sebastes ruberrimus
To 3' (90 cm) long. Orange-red to red-
yellow body. Adults **(A)** have brilliant
yellow eye on rough head. Juveniles **(B)**
have dark eyes and 2 white bands along
the sides that fade in time. Individuals
are long-term residents at specific sites,
60–1,800' (18–540 m) deep.

▲ COPPER ROCKFISH
Sebastes caurinus
To 22" (55 cm) long. Olive-brown to
copper with yellow and white blotches.
Dark bands radiate from the eye. On
rocky reefs, 30–600' (9–180 m) deep.

◄ CHINA ROCKFISH
Sebastes nebulosus
To 17" (42.5 cm) long. Black body
with broad yellow stripe and patches.
Solitary species, resident on reefs,
13–422' (3.9–127 m) deep.

TIGER ROCKFISH ▶
Sebastes nigrocinctus
To 2' (60 cm) long. Pink to red with 5 vertical dark bands. Solitary and territorial, 3–900' (1–270 m) deep.

▲ BLACK ROCKFISH
Sebastes melanops
To 25" (62.5 cm) long. Light to dark grey with dark mottling along upper back and a pale band below lateral line. In schools, often with other rockfish, surface to 1,200' (360 m) deep.

▼ CANARY ROCKFISH
Sebastes pinniger
To 30" (75 cm) long. Orange body **(A)** with white to grey stripe along lateral line, 3 bright stripes across head. Juvenile **(B)** has a prominent dark spot at rear of spiny dorsal fin. In schools, rocky reefs, 60–1,200' (18–360 m) deep.

▼ YELLOWTAIL ROCKFISH
Sebastes flavidus
To 26" (65 cm) long. Olive green to green-brown with pale spots along back, yellow-green on fins. In schools, surface to 1,800' (540 m) deep.

Lingcod, Greenlings

▼ LINGCOD
Ophiodon elongatus
To 5' (1.5 m) long. Weight to 105 lb. (47 kg). Large head, mouth and teeth. Long, tapered body with dark blotches, mottled grey, brown or green. Male guards egg masses in shallows. In kelp beds and on rocky reefs to 6,600' (1,980 m) deep.

KELP GREENLING ▶

Hexagrammos decagrammos

To 2' (60 cm) long. Male **(A)** brown-olive with bright blue spots, female **(B)** light brown, golden to blue, with rows of round orange-brown spots. Small, bushy appendage above each eye. Male guards pale blue to mauve egg mass. In kelp beds and rocky areas, intertidal to 150' (45 m) deep.

▼ PAINTED GREENLING *Oxylebius pictus*

To 10" (25 cm) long. Long, pointed head with 2 pairs of bushy appendages. Dark vertical bars cross body and dorsal fin. Male guards orange egg mass. Sometimes associate with white-spotted anemone (p. 58). On rocky reefs to 162' (49 m) deep.

Perches

▼ STRIPED PERCH

Embiotica lateralis

To 15" (37.5 cm) long. Copper-coloured with about 15 iridescent blue horizontal stripes below lateral line. Common, solitary or in schools, near surface to 70' (21 m) deep.

▼ SHINER PERCH

Cymatogaster aggregata

To 6" (15 cm) long. Small, silvery oval body, compressed, with large scales. Strong dark bars along sides, interrupted by 3 yellow vertical bars. In schools around pilings and floats and in kelp beds, surface to 480' (144 m) deep.

Other Common Bony Fishes

▼ BLACK-EYE GOBE
Coryphopterus nicholsi
To 6" (15 cm) long. Black eyes, black patch at top of forward dorsal fin. Pale to dark tan-orange body with large scales. Territorial, in rock rubble, intertidal to 340' (102 m) deep.

▼ NORTHERN RONQUIL
Ronquilis jordani
To 7" (17.5 cm) long. Elongated body with orange bands or spots below the eyes. Orange-cream to brown, olive green and grey. Long, single dorsal fin. In rock rubble, 10–540' (3–162 m) deep.

◄ PILE PERCH
Rhacochilus vacca
To 17" (42.5 cm) long. Silvery, usually with dark, indistinct vertical bars. Black spot behind mouth. Deeply forked tail fin. Around floats, pilings and reefs, surface to 260' (78 m) deep.

▲ NORTHERN CLINGFISH
Gobiesox maeandricus
To 6" (15 cm) long. Large head and flattened body; adhesive disc on underside. Dark, net-like pattern over body, often with pale band between and below eyes. On undersides of rocks, intertidal to 30' (9 m) deep.

▼ PLAINFIN MIDSHIPMAN
Porichthys notatus
To 15" (37.5 cm) long. Large mouth and head, tapered body **(A)**. Dark grey-brown to purple with rows of luminous white spots. Deposits and guards

yellow-orange clusters of eggs **(B)** under intertidal rocks. On sand–mud, intertidal to 1,200' (360 m).

Warbonnets, Wolf Eels, Gunnels

DECORATED WARBONNET ▶
Chirolophis decoratus
To 16¹/₂" (41 cm) long. Long head with large, bushy appendages centred in front of eyes to back of head. Long body, orange to brown with dark mottling and bars on fins. In crevices and sponges, 5–300' (1.5–90 m) deep.

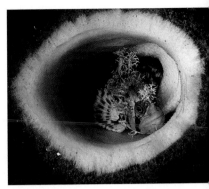

▼ CRESCENT GUNNEL
Pholis laeta
To 10" (25 cm) long. Long and eel-like. Lime-green with crescent-shaped markings along the back. Under rocks and seaweeds, intertidal to 240' (72 m) deep.

▲ MOSSHEAD WARBONNET
Chirolophis nugator
To 6" (15 cm) long. Numerous short, bushy appendages on head. Evenly spaced "eye spots" or bars along dorsal fin. In holes, crevices and empty barnacle shells, intertidal to 200' (60 m) deep.

◀ WOLF-EEL
Anarrichthys ocellatus
To 8' (2.4 m) long. Large head and mouth. Long, tapering body with black "eye spots." Female with dark, rounded head (**A, left**) and male with lighter bulbous head (**A, right**) pair for life and guard eggs in den. Juveniles (**B**) bright orange. Intertidal to 700' (210 m) deep.

Flatfish (Flounders)

▼ C-O SOLE
Pleuronicthys coenosus
To 14" (35 cm) long. Oval body with high sides. Large, dark spot on centre of back resembles the letters *C O*. Large, prominent eyes. On sand and in eelgrass beds, shallows to 1,200' (360 m) deep.

▼ ROCK SOLE
Pleuronectes bilineatus
To 2' (60 cm) long. Black and yellow patches on fins, yellow spots along margins of side. Prominent arch in lateral line. Often rests on fins, unlike most other flounders. In sand or mud, intertidal to 1,500' (450 m) deep.

▼ ENGLISH SOLE
Pleuronectes vetulus
To 22$^{1/2}$" (56 cm) long. Pointed head, large eyes. Slender body, lateral line without high arch. Variable colour patterns. Often partially buried in sand or mud, intertidal to 1,800' (540 m) deep.

Nudibranchs (Sea Slugs)

Phylum Mollusca

Nudibranchs are colourful—sometimes spectacular—favourites of tidepool explorers and divers. Many species have a retractable plume-like gill projection or numerous cerata (protrusions), shaped like fingers, paddles or clubs. Some also have papillae (finger-like projections) or tubercles (bumps) on the body for respiration, camouflage and defence.

Dorid nudibranchs
Features include flattened body, retractable gill plume and rhinophores (paired sensory organs on the head). Dorids lay lacy ribbons of eggs.

▼ LEOPARD (Ringed) DORID
Diaulua sandiegensis
To 3" (7.5 cm) long. Elongated oval body with fine tubercles (bumps). White with dark spots, usually with light to brown rings. On rocks and sponges, intertidal to 115' (35 m) deep.

MONTEREY SEA LEMON ▶
Archidoris montereyensis
To 6" (15 cm) long. Slender. Yellow to orange; dark spots on tubercles (bumps). Feeds on sponges. Usually intertidal, but subtidal to 165' (50 m) deep.

◀ SEA LEMON
Anisodoris nobilis
To 8" (20 cm) long. Yellow to orange; dark spots between tubercles (bumps). White plume. Feeds on sponges. Intertidal, usually subtidal to 750' (225 m) deep.

▼ GIANT WHITE DORID
Archidoris odhneri
To 8" (20 cm) long. Bright white body with many tubercles (bumps). On rocks and sponges, intertidal to 75' (22.5 m) deep.

▲ RED NUDIBRANCH
Rostanga pulchra
To 5/8" (1.5 cm) long. Oval. Red-orange, sometimes with brown to black spots. Lays red ribbons of eggs and feeds on the velvety red sponge (p. 63). Intertidal.

CLOWN DORID ▶
Triopha catalinae
To 6" (15 cm) long. Slender body. White with orange on rhinophores (paired sensory organs on the head), front veil, tubercles (bumps) and gill plume. Feeds on spiral bryozoans (p. 68). Intertidal to 115' (35 m) deep.

▲ BARNACLE NUDIBRANCH
Onchidoris bilamellata
To 3/4" (2 cm) long. Oval. Cream-coloured with pale to dark brown patterns on rough back. Feeds on barnacles. Intertidal.

▼ RED-GILLED (Nanaimo) DORID
Acanthodoris nanaimoensis
To 1 1/4" (3 cm) long. Round. White to grey with long yellow-tipped papillae (finger-like projections); maroon highlights on gill plume and rhinophores (paired sensory organs on the head). Intertidal and shallow subtidal.

▼ YELLOW MARGIN DORID
Cadlina luteomarginata
To 1 3/4" (4.4 cm) long. Oval. White with yellow margin. Low tubercles (bumps), tipped with yellow. Intertidal to 150' (45 m) deep.

◀ HUDSON'S YELLOW MARGIN NUDIBRANCH
Acanthodoris hudsoni
To 3/4" (2 cm) long. Egg-shaped body. White with yellow margin, yellow papillae (finger-like projections). Long rhinophores (paired sensory organs on the head). Intertidal and shallow subtidal.

Dendronotid Nudibranchs
Features include highly branched cerata (appendages) or gill-tufts and sheathed rhinophores (paired sensory organs on the head). Dendronotids lay coiled strings of eggs.

▼ GIANT DENDRONOTID
Dendronotus iris
To 10" (25 cm) long. Long, branched protrusions on back, frontal veil of 4 paired appendages. Colour varies from white to grey, orange or red. White line along foot margin. Common; feeds on tube-dwelling anemone (p. 59). Shallow subtidal.

GIANT RED DENDRONOTID ▶
Dendronotus rufus
To 11" (27.5 cm) long. Long body.
White, often with red-maroon spots.
All appendages have red-maroon tips.
Red-maroon line along foot margin.
On rocks and algae, shallow subtidal.

◀ VARIABLE DENDRONOTID
Dendronotus diversicolor
To 2" (5 cm) long. Slender body.
White to lilac. Top third of gill tufts
and cerata (appendages) white, orange
or both. White stripe down tail from
behind last pair of gill tufts. On rocks
and hydroids, shallow subtidal.

DALL'S DENDRONOTID ▶
Dendronotus dalli
To 5¹/₂" (14 cm) long. Long
white body with branched,
white-tipped appendages.
Feeds on hydroids (pp. 60–61).
On rocks, shallow subtidal.

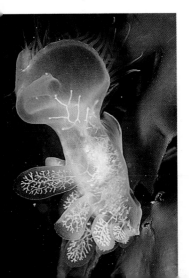

◀ HOODED NUDIBRANCH
Melibe leonina
To 4" (10 cm) long. Slender body. Translucent
white, yellow-brown to green-brown and spotted.
Has paddle-like appendages and a large hood
with 2 fringes of tentacles to capture prey. On
rocks and kelp, intertidal and shallow subtidal.

◄ ORANGE PEEL NUDIBRANCH
Tochuina tetraquetra
To 12" (30 cm) long. Long body. Brilliant yellow-orange with white tubercles (bumps) and white tufts along edges. Feeds on hydroids (p. 60), sea pens (p. 55) and soft corals (p. 56). Shallow subtidal.

PINK TRITONIA ▶
Tritonia diomedea
To 8³/4" (22 cm) long. Broad oval body with gill tufts around edge. White line along margin of foot. Feeds on white and orange sea pens (p. 55). On sand–mud, shallow subtidal.

◄ DIAMOND BACK TRITONIA
Tritonia festiva
To 4" (10 cm) long. Slender body with tufts around edge. White to pink, usually with white diamond pattern on the back. Often feeds on soft corals (p. 56). Low intertidal to 165' (50 m) deep.

Arminacea Nudibranchs

Features include numerous groups or rows of cerata (appendages) or gill-tufts, frontal veil and unsheathed rhinophores (paired sensory organs on the head). They lay coiled strings of eggs.

STRIPED NUDIBRANCH
Armina californica ▶
To 2³/4" (7 cm) long. Smooth brown body with raised longitudinal ridges. No visible cerata (appendages) at edges. Often feeds on orange sea pens (at right in photo). In sand–mud, shallow subtidal to 755' (226 m) deep.

▲ **WHITE-LINED DIRONA**
Dirona albolineata
To 7" (17.5 cm) long. Translucent body with wide front veil. Grey or white to purple with large, flattened, pointed, white-edged appendages. On rocks, intertidal to 115' (35 m) deep.

▲ **GOLD DIRONA**
Dirona aurantia
To 5" (12.5 cm) long. Oval body. Orange with white spots, lines and on tips of bulbous cerata (appendages). Feeds on bryozoans (p. 67). On rocks, kelp and mud, shallow subtidal.

Aeolid Nudibranchs

Features include long oral tentacles, groups or rows of cerata (appendages) on the back, and long, fleshy rhinophores (paired sensory organs on the head).

OPALESCENT NUDIBRANCH ▶
Hermissenda crassicornis
To 2" (5 cm) long. Slender body, numerous cerata (appendages) with white lines, each topped with orange band and white tip. Often has orange areas on back, bordered by blue. On rocks and floats, intertidal to 115' (35 m) deep.

▲ SHAGGY MOUSE
NUDIBRANCH *Aeolidia papillosa*
To 2³/₈" (6 cm) long. Bare back, numerous shaggy appendages crowded along margins. Grey-brown, usually with a large, triangular patch at front of head region. On rocks or mudflats, intertidal to 2,500' (750 m) deep.

▼ THREE-LINED NUDIBRANCH
Flabellina trilineata
To 1³/8" (3.4 cm) long. Slender white body with three white lines down back. Light red to orange appendages in clusters along margins. White rings on the rhinophores (paired sensory organs on the head). Feeds on hydroids. Low intertidal to 65' (20 m) deep.

▼ RED VERRUCOSE NUDIBRANCH *Flabellina verrucosa*
To 4" (10 cm) long. Slender, translucent white body with short, rounded head. Clusters of brick red appendages with white tips. Shallow subtidal.

◄ PEARLY NUDIBRANCH
Flabellina japonica
To 3" (7.5 cm) long. Pearly cream to pink body, bare back with dense cerata (appendages) along margins. On rocks, shallow subtidal.

▼ RED FLABELLINA
Flabellina triophina
To 4" (10 cm) long. Slender, translucent white body with long, pointed head. Red-pink appendages with white tips along margins. Faint bars on rhinophores (paired sensory organs on the head). On rocks, mud or hydroids (p. 60), low intertidal to at least 65' (20 m).

▼ SPANISH SHAWL
Flabellinopsis iodinea
To 1¹/2" (3.8 cm) long. Deep purple body with orange-tipped cerata (appendages). Feeds on hydroids. On rocky exposed coasts, intertidal to 120' (36 m) deep.

Octopus & Squid

Phylum Mollusca

GIAN PACIFIC OCTOPUS ▶

Enteroctopus dofleini
(=Octopus dofleini)

To 16' (5 m) long from top of head to ends of arms. 8 arms of equal length, each 3 to 5 times body length. Skin wrinkled and folded. Animal **(A)** changes colour from pale to dark reddish brown, sometimes mottled. White streak in skin running through each eye, and single white spot in skin in front of eyes. Female guards clusters of eggs the size of rice grains **(B)** attached to roof of den. Intertidal to 1,650' (495 m) deep.

◀ RED OCTOPUS *Octopus rubescens*

To 20" (50 cm) long from top of head to ends of arms, mantle to 4" (10 cm) long. Each arm is 4 times body length. Can be distinguished from giant octopus (above) by 3 papillae (finger-like projections) under each eye and 2 white spots in skin at front of eyes. Found in bottles or empty shells (inset photo), which serve as dens, in sandy and rocky areas, intertidal to 660' (200 m) deep.

◀ STUBBY SQUID *Rossia pacifica*

To 3" (7.5 cm) long from top of head to end of arms, mantle to 1¹/₂" (3.8 cm) long. Body **(A)** has small semicircular fins. Reddish brown with pale underside. Has 2 long tentacles, kept in a sheath and deployed to capture prey. Clusters of round eggs with points on ends opposite attachment **(B)** are laid on rocks. On rocks or in sand–mud (buried in daytime, on surface at night), subtidal, 50–1,215' (15–365 m) deep.

◀ OPALESCENT SQUID

Loligo opalescens

To 11" (27.5 cm) long from top of head to ends of arms, cylindrical mantle to 8" (20 cm) long. 8 short arms, 2 long tentacles. Animal (**A**) changes colour from translucent white to mottled brown and gold. Schools of squid mate in shallow sandy bays and lay clusters of finger-like eggs (**B**). In coastal shallows and offshore surface waters to bottom.

Bivalves & Lampshells

Clams, Mussels, Oysters, Scallops, Cockles & Lampshells

Phylum Mollusca, Phylum Brachiopoda

Bivalves ("two shells") are a class of molluscs, a large, diverse group of animals with soft, unsegmented bodies. The lampshell, while very similar in appearance, is a brachiopod ("arm foot"), a very different animal.

Mussels

Mussel shells are symmetrical, elongated and typically attached in clumps by strong, thin byssus (thread-like secretion). Mussels are common and abundant on floating structures, pilings, and intertidal and subtidal rocks and gravel. There is likely one native species of blue mussel, the most common species in the region— Pacific blue mussel (*Mytilus trossulus*)—and several distinct introduced species of bay and blue mussels. These species are difficult to identify by their shells alone and the situation is complicated by the existence of many hybrids.

▼ PACIFIC BLUE MUSSEL

Mytilus trossulus

To 4$\frac{1}{2}$" (11 cm) long. Elongated, narrow, curved anterior end. Bluish black, often with purplish eroded area. On floating structures, pilings, rocks and gravel, intertidal and subtidal.

MEDITERRANEAN BLUE (Gallo's) MUSSEL

Mytilus galloprovincialis ▼

To 6" (15 cm) long. Broad, triangular fan-shaped black shell, pointed anterior end. Introduced from the Atlantic for aquaculture. On floating structures, pilings, rocks and gravel, intertidal and subtidal.

BLUE MUSSEL ▶
Mytilus edulis
To 4¹/2" (11 cm) long. Elongated, narrow end. Ventral margin straight or somewhat curved. Introduced from the Atlantic for aquaculture. On floating structures, pilings, rocks and gravel, intertidal and subtidal.

◀ CALIFORNIA MUSSEL
Mytilus californianus
To 10" (25 cm) long. Thick shells, pointed at anterior end. Strong ribs run along length of shell, often worn off on larger specimens. Exterior may have tan radial rays. Bright orange meat. On exposed oceanic coasts, intertidal to 330' (100 m) deep.

NORTHERN HORSEMUSSEL ▶
Modiolus modiolus
To 7" (27.5 cm) long. Oval, inflated, length is usually twice the height and width. Purple shell covered with brown, hairy periostracum (thin covering). Often in aggregations in gravel, intertidal to 660' (200 m) deep.

Oysters
The lower left (**A**) shell of the oyster is usually cupped and often attached; the upper right (**B**) shell is flattened and smaller than the lower. The height of oyster shells is measured from the hinge to the outer margin. Only one species of oyster, Olympia oyster, is native to this coast. Three other species have been introduced for aquaculture and some have spawned to seed other beaches. The most common and abundant of these is the Pacific Japanese oyster.

▼ OLYMPIA OYSTER *Ostrea conchaphila*
To 3¹/2" (9 cm) diameter. Round to oval shell, often frilled and fluted. Exterior grey, purple or white. Interior greenish to purple with dark muscle scar. On rocks, intertidal to 33' (10 m).

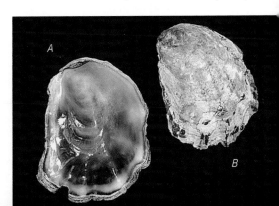

▼ ATLANTIC OYSTER
Crassostrea virginica
To 8" (20 cm) high. Irregular outline. Thick, elongated, ridged shell. Tan to purple, sometimes with ray pattern. Interior white with purple muscle scar. Introduced from the western Atlantic. On firm substrates, intertidal.

◄ PACIFIC JAPANESE OYSTER
Crassostrea gigas
To 12" (30 cm) high. Shell often fluted. Exterior grey-white with purple-black new growth. Interior smooth, white with light-coloured muscle scar. Introduced from Japan. On firm substrates, intertidal.

▼ EUROPEAN FLAT OYSTER
Ostrea edulis
To 3" (7.5 cm) high. Round to pear-shaped with ribs and frilly growth margins. Exterior varies from white to yellow, tan and purple. Interior white. Introduced from Europe. On firm substrates, intertidal.

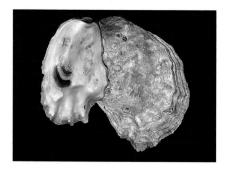

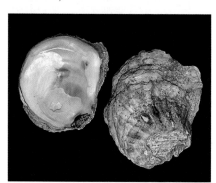

Scallops
Scallops have unequal shells with strong radial ribs and wing-like hinges ("ears"). Eyes around the edge of the mantle are visible between the gaping shells. A scallop may be free-swimming, or attached to a hard surface. Some are heavily encrusted with sponges. There are small fisheries for swimming scallops (mostly the spiny pink) by divers and small trawls.

ROCK SCALLOP ►
Crassadoma gigantea
To 10" (25 cm) high. Thick, round, ribbed shells, often infested with yellow boring sponge (p. 63). Orange mantle with blue eyes. White interior; purple-stained hinge. Cemented to rocks, intertidal to 260' (78 m) deep.

SMOOTH PINK SCALLOP ▸
Chlamys rubida
To 2¹/₂" (6.3 cm) high. Round shells, prominent radial ribs without strong spines. Upper shell pink to red-purple, white or yellow. Lower shell paler. On mud–gravel, 3–665' (1–200 m) deep.

◂ JAPANESE SCALLOP
Mizuhopecten yessoensis
To 9" (22.5 cm) high. Upper (left) shell purple-grey with flattened ribs. Interior margin dark purple. Lower shell white and thick, with rounded ribs.
Introduced from Japan to BC in 1980s for aquaculture.

◂ SPINY PINK SCALLOP
Chlamys hastata
To 3¹/₄" (8 cm) high. Almost round pink shells with fluted margin. Wide, coarse primary ribs with strong spines and several riblets between. On rocky reefs, 7–495' (2–150 m) deep.

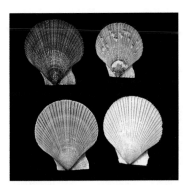

◂ WEATHERVANE SCALLOP
Patinopecten caurinus
To 11" (27.5 cm) high (largest free-swimming scallop in the world). Round shells. Upper shell red-pink to grey with about 17 rounded ribs; lower shell nearly white with about 24 broad, flattened square ribs. In depressions in sand or gravel, 33–660' (10–200 m) deep; sometimes washed ashore.

Cockles

▾ NUTTALL'S HEART COCKLE
Clinocardium nuttallii
To 5¹/₂" (14 cm) long. 34–38 strong ribs, crossed by wavy lines at the margins. Yellow-brown; young mottled with red-brown. Buried near surface of sand, intertidal to 100' (30 m) deep.

Clams

▼ MANILA CLAM
Venerupis philippinarum
To 3" (7.5 cm) long. Elongated oval shells, flattened, with lattice sculpture. Radial ribs are stronger. Colour varies from grey to brown, often streaked, occasionally with angular patterns. Shell interior often stained with yellow and purple. Inside edge of shell is smooth. Short siphons, split at tip. In sand–mud–gravel, high to mid-intertidal.

▼ LITTLENECK CLAM
Protothaca staminea
To 3" (7.5 cm) long. Round to oval shells, inflated, with lattice sculpture. White to brown in colour, often with angular patterns. Interior white. Inside edge of shell has fine teeth. Short siphons, fused at tip. In sand–mud–gravel, mid- to low intertidal, to 35' (10 m) deep.

▲ BUTTER CLAM
Saxidomus gigantea
To 5 1/4" (13 cm) long. Oval to squarish shell with concentric ridges. White to grey; shells gape at posterior (siphon) end. In sand–mud–gravel, mid- to low intertidal, to 130' (39 m) deep.

▲ DARK MAHOGANY CLAM
Nuttallia obscurata
To 2 3/4" (7 cm) long. Thin, flat oval shells. Shiny brown periostracum (shell covering), worn white at hinge. Interior purple, white. Long, separate siphons. Introduced from Japan in 1980s. Buried in sand–mud, high to mid-intertidal.

▲ RAZOR CLAM *Siliqua patula*
To 7" (17.5 cm) long. Long, thin, narrow brittle shells. Rounded ends. Shiny, smooth periostracum (shell covering), olive to brown. Shell interior white with purple, slanting rib to anterior. On surf-exposed sandy beaches, intertidal to 180' (54 m).

GEODUCK CLAM ▶

Panopea abrupta

To 7³/4" (19.5 cm) long. Weight to 10 lb. (4.5 kg) or more. Lives as long as 168 years! Shells are rounded at anterior end, truncated at siphon. Gaping at all sides, due to large body and neck. White shell, thin periostracum (shell covering) at margins. "Shows" of long siphons from body (inset photo) buried to 3' (90 cm) in sand–mud–shell–gravel, intertidal to 350' (105 m) deep.

▲ FAT HORSE CLAM *Tresus capax*

To 7" (17.5 cm) long. Oval shell, length 1¹/2 times the height, gaping at siphon. Hinged from a spoon-shaped socket. Siphons have leathery plates at the tip. Often hosts pea crabs (inset photo). In sand–mud, intertidal to 100' (30 m) deep.

▼ PACIFIC HORSE CLAM

Tresus nuttallii

To 9" (22.5 cm) long. Elongated shell, length more than 1¹/2 times height. Weight to 3 lb. (1.4 kg). Hinged from a spoon-shaped socket. Rarely hosts pea crabs (see fat horse clam, above). Siphons have leathery plates at the tip. In sand–mud, intertidal to 165' (50 m) deep.

▼ (Left) FLAT-TIP PIDDOCK

Penitella penita

To 3" (7.5 cm) long. Elongated shells, each with 3 sections and leathery pads at the end. Small siphon holes in soft rock, mud or clay, intertidal to 72' (22 m) deep.

▼ (Right) ROUGH PIDDOCK

Zirfaea pilsbryi

To 5³/4" (14.4 cm) long. Large white shells with unique sculpture for burrowing. Shells are separated by groove and gape at both ends. Split siphons show at surface, body buried in limestone, shale and hard clay, intertidal to 412' (125 m) deep.

▼ SOFTSHELL CLAM
Mya arenaria
To 6" (15 cm) long. Elongated white
shells with yellow or brown periostracum (thin covering), gaping at
siphon end. Hinged from a spoon-
shaped socket. Introduced from the
Atlantic with oysters. In sand–mud,
intertidal.

▼ NORTHWEST UGLY CLAM
Entodesma navicula
To 6" (15 cm) long. Elongated and
variable shaped shell covered with red-
brown periostracum (thin covering),
which cracks when dried. In crevices,
intertidal to 65' (20 m) deep.

▲ BALTIC MACOMA
Macoma balthica
To 1 1/2" (3.8 cm) long. Oval shells,
often pink, may be blue, orange or yellow. In sand–mud and eelgrass beds,
intertidal to 130' (39 m) deep.

▲ BENT-NOSE MACOMA
Macoma nasuta
To 3" (7.5 cm) long. Thin white shells
bend to the right near the pointed
posterior (siphon) end. In sand,
intertidal to 165' (50 m) deep.

GREEN FALSE-JINGLE ▶
Pododesmus macroschisma
To 5 1/4" (13 cm) long. Thin, round
shells. Lower shell has pear-shaped
hole for a short, thick byssus (thread-
like secretion) fixed with a calcareous
attachment. On rocks, intertidal to
295' (88 m) deep.

Lampshells
Phylum Brachiopoda
The lampshell looks like a bivalve mollusc, but is a brachiopod with 2 shells and a soft body. It attaches to the bottom by a fleshy stalk that protrudes through the shell, and gathers food by sweeping the water with an arm-like structure.

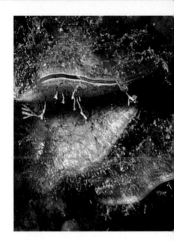

LAMPSHELL *Terebratalia transversa* ▶
To 1¹/₄" (3 cm) long. Smooth to prominently ribbed shells with tan to brown periostracum (thin covering). On rocks and rock faces, intertidal to 5,575' (1,672 m) deep.

Snails, Limpets & Abalone
Phylum Mollusca

Snails, limpets and abalone are single-shelled animals, all members of the gastropod ("belly foot") class. They are quite diverse in form.

Snails

▼ RED TURBAN
Astraea gibberosa
To 3" (7.5 cm) high, 4¹/₂" (11 cm) diameter. Squat, reddish-brown shell. Often covered with coralline algae (p. 76). Whorls have bumpy ridges. Base is flat and furrowed. Pearly operculum ("trap door"). Intertidal to 260' (78 m) deep.

▼ BLACK TURBAN
Tegula funebralis
To 1¹/₄" (3 cm) diameter. Thick black-purple shell, low cone with 4 whorls. Feeds on seaweeds. Common and abundant on rocks, intertidal.

PURPLE-RING TOPSNAIL
Calliostoma annulatum ▼
To 1¹/₄" (3 cm) high. Conical shell with 8 to 9 whorls. Orange-yellow with bright purple-violet bands. On rocks along open coasts, intertidal to 100' (30 m) deep.

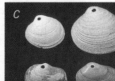

◄ BLUE TOPSNAIL
Calliostoma ligatum
To 1" (2.5) diameter. Brown shell with light tan spiral ridges, worn patches show pearly blue inner layer. Rounded whorls and aperture. Rocky areas, intertidal to 100' (30 m) deep.

SPINY TOPSNAIL ▶
Cidarina cidaris
To 1½" (3.8 cm) high. Rounded, beaded whorls, longitudinal ridges. Exterior grey, whitish when worn. Interior pearly. Common on rocks, 50' (15 m) and deeper.

◄ HAIRY OREGON TRITON
Fusitriton oregonensis
To 6" (15 cm) high. About 6 whorls with axial riblets, spiralling pairs of threads. Thick, shaggy, grey-brown periostracum (shell covering). On rocks, intertidal to 295' (88 m) deep.

LEWIS' MOONSNAIL ▶
Euspira lewisii
To 5½" (14 cm) high. Large, globular shell, cream-coloured with thin brown periostracum (covering). Horny operculum ("trap door"), tan to brown, seals body in shell. Soft body (A) translucent brown, not blotched. Lays eggs in smooth, distinctive sand covered egg collar (B). Drills and feeds on clams, leaving distinctive drill hole (C). In sand–mud, intertidal to 165' (50 m) deep.

ALEUTIAN MOONSNAIL ▶
Cryptonatica aleutica
To 2 1/2" (6.3 cm) high. Shell cream to brown in colour. Calcareous operculum ("trap door"). Soft body, cream-coloured with rusty red to maroon blotches. In sand–mud, intertidal to 1,500' (450 m) deep.

▼ FRILLED DOGWINKLE
Nucella lamellosa
To 3 1/4" (8 cm) high. Variable form, smooth (on exposed beaches) to wrinkled. Up to 12 axial frills. Banded shell, white to brown in colour. Lays clusters of stalked, pointed yellow egg capsules. Outer lip broadly flared with 3 rounded teeth. Intertidal to shallow subtidal.

▲ SPINDLE (Dire) WHELK
Lirabuccinum dirum
To 2" (5 cm) high. Thick, strong shell. 9 to 11 low, rounded axial ribs. Numerous unsymmetrical spiral threads. Dull grey. On rocks, intertidal.

▼ LEAFY HORNMOUTH
Ceratostoma foliatum
To 3 1/2" (9 cm) high. Large tooth projects from aperture. White or white with brown bands; 3 wing-like projections or frills. Lays clusters of yellow egg capsules. Intertidal to 215' (65 m).

▼ CHANNELED DOGWINKLE
Nucella canaliculata
To 1 1/2" (3.8 cm) high. 14 to 16 slender spiral ridges, separated by deep furrows. White to grey. Feeds on barnacles. On rocks, intertidal.

▲ MUDFLAT SNAIL
Battallaria cumingi
To 1¹/4" (3 cm) high. Small, elongated shell. 8 to 9 grey whorls with brown-beaded spiral ridges. Abundant on sand–mud, mid- to low intertidal.

▲ PURPLE OLIVE
Olivella biplicata
To 1¹/4" (3 cm) high. Long, smooth, shiny shell. Whitish to purple. Often leaves trail in the sand. On exposed sandy beaches, low intertidal to 150' (45 m) deep.

Limpets
The keyhole limpet can be identified by a hole near the apex (peak) of the shell. The "true" limpet has a single cone-shaped shell. Many limpets are preyed upon by sea stars, and show an escape response that may include twisting, releasing and falling, or "flight." Limpets graze on algae. They are often found in the shade or on the underside of rocks, intertidal and shallow subtidal.

▼ ROUGH KEYHOLE LIMPET
Diodora aspera
To 2³/4" (7 cm) across. Oval shell with lattice sculpture. Apex (peak) slightly off-centre with circular opening at top. Scale worm (p. 66) may be found in underside groove. On rocks, low inter-tidal and shallow subtidal.

▼ WHITECAP LIMPET
Acmaea mitra
To 1³/8" (3.4 cm) diameter, 1¹/4" (3 cm) high. Thick round shell with cen-tral apex (peak). White or overgrown with coralline algae (p. 76), on which it feeds. On exposed coasts, intertidal and shallow subtidal.

PLATE LIMPET *Tectura scutum* ▼
To 1 ³/4" (4.5 cm) diameter. Low, flat-tened shell with off-centre apex (peak). Green-grey with light and dark streaks or checkerboard pattern. Intertidal and shallow subtidal.

MASK LIMPET ▶
Tectura persona
To 2" (5 cm) diameter. Oval shell, smooth margin. Exterior blue-grey, brown and black at top, speckled with white. Interior blue-white with dark margin, often with white spots and a dark mask-like stain behind the apex (peak). On rocks, high intertidal.

◀ SHIELD LIMPET
Lottia pelta
To 1³/₄" (4.5 cm) diameter, ⁵/₈" (1.5 cm) high. Oval shell, apex (peak) nearly at centre. Irregular ribbing. Exterior grey; irregular white radial stripes form a net pattern. Interior blue-white with brown spot. In mussel beds, often with sea palm (p. 75), sometimes on feather boa kelp (p. 75), intertidal.

Abalone

▼ RIBBED LIMPET
Lottia digitalis
To 1¹/₄" (3 cm) diameter. Elongated oval shell with apex (peak) near anterior. Prominent ribs radiate from apex. Exterior grey with olive-green bands. On exposed coasts, high intertidal and splash zones.

▼ NORTHERN ABALONE
Haliotis kamtschatkana
To 7" (17.5 cm) long. Thin, elongated-oval shell with irregular surface and 3 to 6 open holes. Interior iridescent white. In kelp beds or on rocks, intertidal to 50' (15 m) deep.

Chitons

Phylum Mollusca

These oval, flattened animals have 8 overlapping plates (valves) bound together with a leathery girdle. Most chitons live hidden under rocks, intertidal and shallow subtidal, and a few are common in tidepools.

▼ LEATHER CHITON
Katherina tunicata
To 3" (7.5 cm) long. Smooth girdle covering about 2/3 of the plates. Brown to black. On rocks in current and wave-swept areas, mid-intertidal.

▼ LINED (RED) CHITON
Tonicella lineata
To 2" (5 cm) long. Smooth, dark girdle, often banded. Red to orange-pink valves with dark zigzag lines edged with white. On rocks, grazing on coralline algae (p. 76), 3–65' (1–20 m) deep.

▼ BLUE-LINE CHITON
Tonicella undocaerulea
To 2" (5 cm) long. Smooth, banded girdle. Light orange to pink valves with concentric white zigzag lines, brilliant blue zigzag lines. On rocks, grazing on coralline algae (p. 76), 3–165' (1–50 m) deep.

▼ MOSSY CHITON
Mopalia muscosa
To 2¾" (7 cm) long. Girdle has small notch in the rear, stout, stiff hairs along edges. Valves dull, often worn, dark brown or grey to black. Valves may have growths of seaweed or barnacles. On rocks, intertidal.

▼ MERTEN'S CHITON
Lepidozona mertensii
To 1¹/2" (3.8 cm) long. Girdle has low, smooth scales with yellow and reddish bands. Valves are reddish or green-purple, with strong white lines. On rocks, intertidal to 300' (90 m) deep.

GIANT PACIFIC CHITON ▶
Cryptochiton stelleri
To 13" (32.5 cm) long. Body
(A) has large plates, called
butterfly shells **(B)**, complete-
ly covered by brown to reddish brown girdle. Underside
yellow with broad, edible
foot. Intertidal to 65' (20 m)
deep.

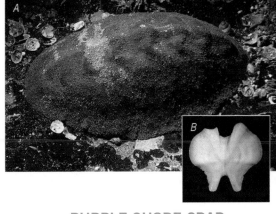

Crabs & Shrimp

Phylum Arthropoda

Crabs

▼ HAIRY SHORE CRAB
Hemigrapsus oregonensis
Carapace to 2" (5 cm) wide. Hairy legs,
body grey to dark green, white or mottled. Under rocks, intertidal.

▼ PURPLE SHORE CRAB
Hemigrapsus nudus
Carapace to 2¹/₄" (5.6 cm) wide.
Square carapace, typically purple with
dark spots on claws, but may be olive
or red-brown. Walking legs smooth,
not hairy. Under rocks, intertidal.

▼ BLACK-CLAWED CRAB
Lophopanopeus bellus bellus
Carapace to 1¹/₂" (3.8 cm) wide.
Thick, smooth, heavy dark claws.
Body colour varies from purple to grey
to dark brown. Under rocks, intertidal.

◀ DUNGENESS CRAB
Cancer magister
Carapace to 10" (25 cm) wide, widest at tenth and largest tooth. Carapace grey-brown and purple, legs grey-brown with orange, underside yellow. Male (inset) has V-shaped abdomen, female has U-shaped abdomen. In sand–mud or eelgrass, intertidal to 750' (225 m) deep.

▼ SLENDER CANCER CRAB *Cancer gracilis*
Carapace to 4 1/2" (11 cm) wide. Broad marginal teeth outlined in white, legs purple, claws purple with white tips. Often mistaken for Dungeness crab. In sand–mud, intertidal to 470' (140 m).

▼ HAIRY CANCER CRAB
Cancer oregonensis
Carapace to 2" (5 cm) wide. Dull red, circular carapace. Short, hairy legs. Claws have black-tipped pincers. In small holes and empty giant barnacle shells, low intertidal to 1,335' (400 m) deep.

▼ RED ROCK CRAB
Cancer productus
Carapace to 8" (20 cm) wide. Fan-shaped carapace is brick red. Claws have black-tipped pincers. Juvenile's colour variable (inset photo), white to dark red streaked with white. In eel-grass, gravel and rocky areas, intertidal to 260' (78 m) deep.

SLENDER DECORATOR CRAB *Oregonia gracilis* ▼
Carapace to 1 1/2" (3.8 cm) wide. Triangular carapace with 2 equally long horns. Long, slender walking legs. Grey or tan body, highly decorated with sponges, hydroids, algae and other organisms. On rocks, intertidal to 1,430' (430 m) deep.

▼ NORTHERN KELP CRAB
Pugettia producta
Carapace to 3¹/₂" (9 cm) wide. Smooth carapace, red to olive in colour. Front margin straight or slightly curved between lateral teeth. Pointed legs. Underside yellow to scarlet. In kelp beds and on pilings, intertidal to 240' (72 m) deep.

▼ SLENDER KELP CRAB
Pugettia gracilis
Carapace to 1³/₈" (3.4 cm) wide. Smooth carapace, brown, yellow or red. Front margin indented between teeth. Ends of claws are blue with red tips. On eelgrass, kelp and rocks, intertidal to 460' (138 m) deep.

BROWN BOX CRAB ▶
Lopholithodes foraminatus
Carapace to 8" (20 cm) wide. Boxy shape. Bumpy body, tan to red-brown. Unique circular holes between first walking legs and claws. In sand–mud, low intertidal to 1,800' (550 m) deep.

▼ SHARP-NOSE CRAB
Scyra acutafrons
Carapace to 1³/₄" (4.4 cm) wide. 2 flattened, leaf-like horns. Short, stout walking legs and large, long claws. Rocky areas, low intertidal to 720' (215 m) deep.

▼ PUGET SOUND KING CRAB
Lopholithodes mandtii
Carapace to 12" (30 cm) wide. Box-like body with 4 large bumps on top. Colour is a mix of bright red, purple, orange. Juveniles are a uniform bright red. On rocky reefs in currents, shallow subtidal to 450' (135 m) deep.

◄ HEART LITHODE
Phyllolithodes papillosus
Carapace to 3¹/2" (9 cm) wide.
Triangular carapace with raised heart-shaped outline. Body grey to brown
with orange markings. Legs have long,
flattened spines and white "socks."
Rocky reefs, shallow subtidal to 600'
(180 m) deep.

HAIRY LITHODE ►
Hapalogaster mertensii
Carapace to 1¹/2" (3.8 cm) wide.
Flattened, hairy brown body with flat,
soft abdomen. Often under rocks in
currents, intertidal to 180' (54 m) deep.

▼ GRANULAR CLAW CRAB
Oedignathus inermis
Carapace to 1¹/2" (3.8 cm) wide. Pear-shaped carapace with flattened abdomen.
Large right claw with blue granules. In
crevices and empty giant barnacle shells,
intertidal to 60' (18 m) deep.

▲ GOLF-BALL LITHODE
Rhinolithodes wosnessenskii
Carapace to 2¹/2" (6.3 cm) wide.
Triangular carapace with semi-circular
depression that forms a ball shape.
Grey body with orange and white
markings. On rock walls, subtidal
20–240' (6–72 m) deep.

◄ RED FUR CRAB
Acantholithodes hispidus
Carapace to 2¹/2" (6.3 cm) wide. Soft,
spiny, hairy body dappled with red,
brown and white. Claws bright red-orange. In sand–mud and rocky areas,
intertidal to 540' (162 m) deep.

◀ FLARING TURTLE CRAB
Cryptolithodes sitchensis
Carapace to 4" (10 cm) wide. Oval
carapace covers legs and smooth
claws. Rostrum (horn) flares at tip.
Colours and patterns variable with
orange, red and grey. On rocks, low
intertidal to 60' (18 m) deep.

BUTTERFLY CRAB
Cryptolithodes typicus ▶
Carapace to 3" (7.5 cm) wide. Oval
carapace covers legs and smooth claws.
Rostrum (horn) narrows at tip. White
and black with patterns and shades of
grey, pink and brown. On rocks, low
intertidal to 150' (45 m) deep.

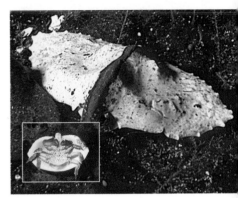

▼ PORCELAIN CRAB
Petrolisthes eriomerus
Carapace to 3/4" (2 cm) wide. Flattened,
dark brown body. Claws are broad and
flat with bright blue markings. Drops
legs when disturbed. Under rocks,
intertidal to 280' (85 m) deep.

▲ SQUAT LOBSTER
Munida quadraspina
Carapace to 3" (7.5 cm) long, body to
5" (12.5 cm) long. Lobster-like animal
with long, slender claws. Red-brown to
orange body. On or swimming above
mud bottoms, subtidal 40–4,800'
(1,440 m) deep.

ORANGE HERMIT CRAB ▶
Elassochirus gilli
Carapace to 1 1/2" (3.8 cm) long.
Smooth, orange legs and claws, white
spots at joints. Rocky areas, intertidal
to 665' (200 m) deep.

WIDEHAND HERMIT CRAB ▶
Elassochirus tenuimanus
Carapace to 1 1/2" (3.8 cm) long. Large, flattened right claw with a wide "hand." Reddish brown to purple-blue on walking legs. On sand, mud, shell and gravel, intertidal to 1,275' (380 m) deep.

◀ BERING HERMIT CRAB
Pagurus beringanus
Carapace to 1" (2.5 cm) long. Brown claws with red bumps and spines; pale blue walking legs with red bands and spots. Often found in large, heavy shell. In rocky areas, intertidal to 1,195' (358 m).

Shrimp

▼ BROKEN BACK SHRIMP
Heptacarpus kincaidi
Carapace to 1/4" (6 mm) long, body to 1 3/8" (3.4 cm) long. Prominent hump on back. Transparent body with red and yellow bars; white midrib on rostrum (horn). On rocks, at base of snakelock or painted anemone (pp. 59, 57), subtidal 33–600' (10–180 m) deep.

▲ CANDYSTRIPE SHRIMP
Lebbeus grandimanus
Carapace to 3/8" (9 mm) long, body to 1 3/8" (3.4 cm) long. Transparent body with brilliant bands of red, yellow and blue. At base of snakelock, painted (pp. 59, 57), and other anemones, subtidal 20–590' (6–177 m) deep.

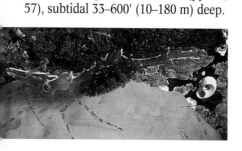

COONSTRIPE (Dock) SHRIMP ▶
Pandalus danae
Carapace to 1 1/4" (3 cm) long, body to 5 1/2" (14 cm) long. Translucent body with red-brown irregular stripes, thin white lines and many fine blue spots. On pilings or rocks and in kelp, intertidal to 605' (181 m) deep.

SPOT PRAWN ▶
Pandalus platyceros
Carapace to 2³/8" (6 cm) long, body to 10" (25 cm) long (females largest). Red body with conspicuous white spots, paired on the first and fifth abdominal sections. Carapace in head region has white bars. Rocky areas, intertidal to 1,600' (480 m) deep.

◀ SPINY PINK SHRIMP
Pandalus borealis eous
Carapace to 1" (2.5 cm) long, body to 5" (12.5 cm) long. Fine red dots over translucent body; spines along back and at posterior of third and fourth body segments. Soft sand–mud, subtidal 55–4,535' (16.5–1,360 m) deep.

BLUE MUD SHRIMP ▶
Upogebia pugettensis
To 6" (15 cm) long, ¹/2" (1 cm) high. Speckled, tan-grey to blue-grey. Hairy legs; fan-shaped tail. First pair of legs unequal in size, with small claws. Burrows in sand–mud or mud–gravel, intertidal.

GHOST SHRIMP
Neotrypaea californiensis ▶
To 4⁵/8" (11.5 cm) long, ³/4" (2 cm) high. Smooth, slender body, pink, orange and yellow in colour. White, hairless claws are unequal in size. Male has huge claw. Makes U-shaped burrow; leaves volcano-like mound at entrance. In sand–mud, intertidal.

Small Crustaceans

Barnacles, Isopods & Amphipods

Phylum Arthropoda

Barnacles

▾ ACORN BARNACLE
Balanus glandula
To $3/4$" (2 cm) high, $3/4$" (2 cm) diameter. Small, white volcano-like shells and plates. Common on rocks, floats and pilings, intertidal.

▴ THATCHED BARNACLE
Semibalanus cariosus
To $2^{3}/8$" (6 cm) diameter, $2^{1}/2$" (6.3 cm) high. Ribbed wall, "thatched" with downward pointing projections. White to dirty grey. Sometimes tall and crowded. On rocks, intertidal and subtidal to 180' (54 m) deep.

▾ GOOSE BARNACLE
Pollicipes polymerus
To $1^{1}/8$" (2.8 cm) wide at the crown, stalk to 6" (15 cm) high. Grows in clumps. Individual is a leathery stalk topped with 5 large plates and numerous small plates. On rocks, intertidal to 100' (30 m) deep.

▾ BROWN BARNACLE
Chthamalus dalli
To $1/4$" (6 mm) diameter, $1/8$" (3 mm) high. Grey-brown shell; brown cover plates form a cross. Highest barnacle in the intertidal.

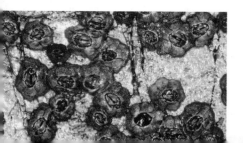

▾ GIANT BARNACLE
Balanus nubilus
To 4" (10 cm) diameter, 5" (12.5 cm) high. Often in large clumps, 12" (30 cm) or more diameter. 2 of the 4 closing plates are hooked. On rocks, intertidal to 300' (90 m) deep.

▾ PELAGIC GOOSE
BARNACLE *Lepas anatifera*
To 2³/4" (7 cm) wide at crown, 8" (20 cm) long. Purple-brown on fleshy stalk. White plates with fine striations and orange along edges. On floating objects and on floating structures at surface.

Isopods, Amphipods

▾ KELP ISOPOD
Idotea wosnesenskii
To 1³/8" (3.4 cm) long. Elongated, flattened segmented body with thick antennae and 7 pairs of walking legs. Black, tan, pink-red and green. In mussels and on kelp and coralline algae (pink specimens), mid-intertidal to 50' (15 m) deep.

BEACH HOPPER (Amphipod)
Traskorchestia traskiana ▾
To ³/4" (2 cm) long. Dark grey body, transparent antennae. In seaweed drift, gravel, rocky and sand beaches, high intertidal.

▾ SKELETON SHRIMP
(Caprellid Amphipod)
Caprella sp.
To 2" (5 cm) long. Thin, elongated shrimp-like body, often bent in a loop to move. Clings to eelgrass (p. 77), hydroids (p. 60) and seaweeds, intertidal and shallow subtidal.

Sea Stars, Basket Star & Brittle Star *Phylum Echinodermata*

The echinoderms ("spiny-skinned") animals have a variety of shapes (sea stars, sea urchins, sand dollars, sea lilies) but consistently have radial symmetry; adults have 5-part symmetry. They are foragers of live and dead animals, seaweed drift and bottom sediments, and as such they play an important role in marine ecology.

Sea stars

Most sea stars have 5 symmetrical arms (or "rays"), but the number varies by species. The animal has cylindrical tube feet on the underside of each arm, which it uses for locomotion, and a mouth on the underside.

▼ OCHRE STAR
Pisaster ochraceus
Radius to 10" (25 cm). Thick, stiff body; 5 arms. Purple or orange with network of white spines. Feeds on mussels, barnacles, limpets and snails. Often found in clusters, in tidepools to 290' (87 m) deep.

MOTTLED STAR ▶
Evasterias troschelii
Radius to 11.8" (30 cm). Small disc; 5 long, tapered arms.

Colour variable from rust to brown, orange and blue-grey. Eats a variety of bivalves, chitons, barnacles and sea squirts (p. 69). On rocks or cobble, intertidal to 246' (75 m) deep.

PAINTED STAR ▶
Orthasterias koehleri
Radius to 10" (25 cm). 5 long arms with promi-

nent white or purple spines, reddish banding and white-cream patches. Often feeds on bivalves. On sand–shell to rock, intertidal to 755' (230 m) deep.

PINK STAR ▶
Pisaster brevispinus
Radius to 12 1/2" (32 cm). Large, stiff body; 5 long arms. Pink to grey. Feeds on bivalves and snails. On soft surfaces, intertidal to 420' (128 m) deep.

◄ SIX RAY STAR *Leptasterias* spp.
Radius to 2" (5 cm). Highly variable and difficult to identify as individual species. 6 arms, broad at the base, tapering quickly to blunt tips. Colour varies from grey to green, pink, purple and orange. Under rocks and in crevices, intertidal to 150' (45 m) deep.

BAT STAR *Asterina miniata* ▶
Radius to 4" (10 cm). Rough, granular surface; 5 short arms with web-footed appearance. Colourful with red, blue, yellow, green and brown. On rocks or sand–mud on exposed coast, intertidal to 991' (302 m) deep.

◄ LEATHER STAR
Dermasterias imbricata
Radius to 6" (15 cm). Smooth, slick, leathery surface; 5 short, thick arms. Upper surface grey with patches of red, brown and purple. On rocks, intertidal to 300' (90 m) deep.

▼ VERMILION STAR
Mediaster aequalis
Radius to 4" (10 cm). Large, flat disc; 5 tapered arms. Surface covered with vermilion plates. On rocks, intertidal to 961' (293 m) deep.

▲ COOKIE STAR
Ceramaster patagonicus
Radius to 3 1/4" (8 cm). Pentagonal disc; 5 short, pointed arms. Slightly inflated. Granular surface with marginal plates. Cream to orange. On rocks to mud, subtidal, 33–804' (10–245 m) deep.

▼ CUSHION STAR

Pteraster tesselatus
Radius to 4³/4" (11.8 cm). Broad disc;
5 short, stubby arms. Slightly elevated
central pore on topside, rather than
sieve plate. Yellow to tan and grey,
sometimes with pattern. On rocks,
subtidal, 20–1,430' (6–436 m) deep.

▼ FAT BLOOD STAR

Henricia sanguinolenta
Radius to 9¹/4" (23 cm). Long, tapered
arms, fat and creased where they leave
the disc. Nearly white, lavender or pale
orange. On rocks to mud, subtidal,
50–1,700' (15–528 m) deep.

◄ ROSE STAR

Crossaster papposus
Radius to 7" (17.5 cm). Soft bodied;
8–16 arms. Purple body with concentric rings of red, orange, white or yellow. On rocks, intertidal to 3,937'
(1,200 m) deep.

▲ WRINKLED STAR

Pteraster militaris
Radius to 3" (7.5 cm). Soft, fleshy
wrinkled body with large upper central
pore. Cream to yellow to pink. Feeds
on sponges and hydrocorals (p. 54).
On rocks to mud, subtidal, 30–3,609'
(9–1,100 m) deep.

▼ BLOOD STAR

Henricia leviuscula
Radius to 6¹/4" (16 cm). Long, thin
arms from small disc; 3 rows of plates
along lower side of each arm. Orange
to brick red, sometimes with grey
patch. On rocks, intertidal to 1,435'
(431 m) deep.

SPINY RED STAR *Hippasteria spinosa* ▶
Radius to 6⅝" (17 cm). Broad disc; 5 short arms with prominent tapering spines over the body. Red to orange. Feeds on orange sea pens (p. 00) and anemones. On rocks, sand to shell, subtidal, 33–1,680' (10–512 m) deep.

◀ SPINY MUDSTAR
Luidia foliolata
Radius to 12" (30 cm). Small disc; 5 long, flattened arms with white marginal spines. Dull grey-brown, underside with yellow-orange tube feet. In sand–mud, intertidal to 2,011' (613 m) deep.

LONG RAY STAR ▶
Stylasterias forreri
Radius to 13" (32.5 cm). Small disc with very long arms. Black or grey with grey wreaths of pincers and white spines. On rocks to sand–mud, 20–1,745' (6–523 m) deep.

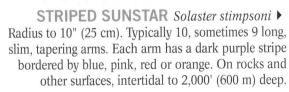

◀ SUNFLOWER STAR
Pycnopodia helianthoides
Radius to 18" (45 cm). Soft body, broad disc; up to 24 arms. Abundant surface spines, pincers and gills. Fast-moving. On many surfaces, intertidal to 1,435' (431 m) deep.

STRIPED SUNSTAR *Solaster stimpsoni* ▶
Radius to 10" (25 cm). Typically 10, sometimes 9 long, slim, tapering arms. Each arm has a dark purple stripe bordered by blue, pink, red or orange. On rocks and other surfaces, intertidal to 2,000' (600 m) deep.

◀ MORNING SUNSTAR
Solaster dawsoni
Radius to 8" (20 cm). Broad disc; 8–15 long, tapering arms. Brown-orange, occasionally red or mottled brown-orange. Often preys on other sea stars. On rocks, gravel and sand, intertidal to 1,380' (414 m) deep.

Basket Star, Brittle Star

▼ BASKET STAR
Gorgonocephalus eucnemis
To 18" (45 cm) diameter. 5 arms branch repeatedly into hundreds of branchlets. White to tan with pink to orange-red mottling. Subtidal, 33–6,600' (10–1.980 m) deep.

▼ DAISY BRITTLE STAR
Ophiopholis aculeata
Arms to 6" (15 cm), from a small disc, 3/4" (2 cm) diameter. Scallop-edged disc. Long, broad arms with blunt spines. Variable colours and patterns of pink, red, orange, blue, green, grey and black. Under rocks or in kelp holdfasts, intertidal to 6,352' (2,000 m) deep.

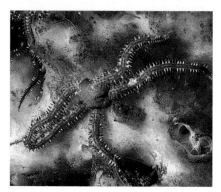

Sea Urchins, Sea Cucumbers, Feather Star & Sand Dollar

Phylum Echinodermata

Sea Urchins

▼ RED SEA URCHIN
Strongylocentrotus franciscanus
Shell to 6" (15 cm) diameter, 2" (5 cm) high. Abundant long, sharp spines. Red to purple-black. On rocky shores and kelp beds, intertidal to 410' (125 m) deep.

▲ GREEN SEA URCHIN
Strongylocentrotus droebachiensis
Shell to 3 1/2" (9 cm) diameter, 1 1/2" (3.8 cm) high. Short, crowded spines, equal in length, are pale green, sometimes purple. Dark tube feet. On rocks, intertidal to 3,795' (1,138 m) deep.

▾ PURPLE SEA URCHIN
Strongylocentrotus purpuratus
Shell to 3¹/₂" (9 cm) diameter, 1³/₄"
(4.4 cm) high. Short purple spines to 1"
(2.5 cm) in the intertidal and 2³/₈" (6
cm) in the subtidal. On exposed rocky
coasts, intertidal to 525' (157 m) deep.

Sea Cucumbers

▾ ORANGE SEA CUCUMBER
Cucumaria miniata
To 8" (20 cm) long. Elongated orange
body with rows of brown tube feet.
Head has 10 tentacles of equal length.
Under rocks or in crevices in currents,
intertidal to 740' (222 m) deep.

▴ WHITE SEA CUCUMBER
Eupentacta quinquesemita
To 4" (10 cm) long. Elongated body. 8
large and 2 smaller tentacles. White
body, sometimes yellow or pink at base
of tentacles. Between rocks in currents,
intertidal to 180' (54 m) deep.

▴ CALIFORNIA
SEA CUCUMBER
Parastichopus californicus
To 20" (50 cm) long. Elongated, fleshy
appendages, both large and small.
Circle of 20 short, bushy feeding
tentacles. Body red to mottled brown-
red. In a variety of habitats, intertidal
to 820' (246 m) deep.

CREEPING PEDAL
SEA CUCUMBER
Psolus chitonoides ▸
To 2³/₄" (7 cm) long. Oval, dome-like
body with overlapping plates. Orange,
with 10 brilliant orange tentacles. On
rocks, intertidal to 810' (243 m) deep.

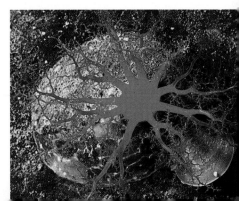

Feather Star or Sea Lily

The animal's 10 feathery arms capture food in the currents. A ring of jointed appendages attach to rocks.

▼ FEATHER STAR
Florometra serratissima
To 10" (25 cm) high. 10 feathery arms radiate from a plate, attached to the rocks by a ring of appendages. Tan to reddish tan. On rock walls, usually in clusters, subtidal, 33–4,108' (10–1,252 m) deep.

Sand Dollar

▼ SAND DOLLAR (Eccentric)
Dendraster excentricus
To 4" (10 cm) diameter. Short, flattened skeleton and spines on both surfaces. Star-shaped series of holes, resembling the petals of a flower, where respiratory tube feet stick out. Lavender-grey, red-brown to purple-black. White shell is often washed up on shore. On sand, intertidal to 130' (39 m) deep.

Corals & Anemones

Phylum Cnidaria

Hydrocorals

The hydrocorals are named for their calcareous skeletons, which resemble those of true corals. They occur in many forms.

▼ ENCRUSTING HYDROCORAL *Stylantheca* spp.
Crust to $1/8$" (3 mm) thick, to 6" (15 cm) or more across. Thin, hard, smooth colony with small holes occupied by polyps. Often confused with smooth (no holes) coralline algae (p. 76). Low intertidal to 100' (30 m).

PINK HYDROCORAL
Stylaster venustus ▼
To 3" (7.5 cm) high, 3' (1 m) or more diameter. Mass of thickly branching colonies. Rose pink to faded violet branches with white tips. On clean, current-swept rocks, 40–80' (12–24 m) deep.

Sea Pens

Sea pens are octocorals, each polyp with 8 tentacles. They can retract fully into the sea bottom. Sea pens can often be seen in the shallows by divers, or from boats or wharves.

▼ ORANGE SEA PEN
Ptilosarcus gurneyi
To 18" (45 cm) high, 4" (10 cm) across in spots. Fleshy orange stalk and branches with many polyps. Bioluminescent (glows when disturbed). Anchored in sand–mud, intertidal to 330' (100 m) deep.

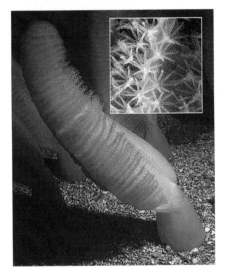

▲ WHITE SEA PEN
Virgularia sp.
To 12" (30 cm) high, 4" (10 cm) across in spots. Thin white stalk and slender, delicate white branches. Anchored in sand–mud, 50' (15 m) and deeper. Eaten by the pink tritonia nudibranch (p. 22).

▼ SEA WHIP
Balticina septentrionalis
To 8' (2.4 m) high, to 3" (7.5 cm) across in spots. Slender, short white branches on a thick supporting rod. In sand–mud, 65' (20 m) and deeper.

Zoanthids, Cup Corals, Club Anemones

ZOANTHIDS
Epizoanthus scotinus ▼
To 2" (5 cm) high, colonies to at least 3' (1 m) across. Hundreds of orange-yellow individual polyps grow from a common base. On rocks, intertidal and subtidal.

TAN CUP CORAL ▶
Caryophyllia alaskensis
To 1/2" (1 cm) high, 1" (2.5 cm) diameter. Beige or brown to pink polyp with long, slender tentacles. On rocks, shallow subtidal.

▲ SEA STRAWBERRY SOFT CORAL *Gersemia rubiformis*
Lumps to 6" (15 cm) high and wide. Soft, firm colonies of polyps, each an octocoral (has 8 tentacles) with delicate side branches. Cream or pink to red. Eaten by nudibranchs. Juvenile basket stars (p. 52) settle on this coral. On rocks and current-swept areas, rarely intertidal, subtidal to at least 65' (20 m) deep.

▲ ORANGE CUP CORAL
Balanophyllia elegans
To 1/2" (1 cm) high, 1/2" (1 cm) diameter. Solitary calcareous cup, bright orange, polyp with nearly transparent tentacles. On rocks, intertidal to 65' (20 m) deep.

◀ STRAWBERRY ANEMONE
Corynactis californica
To 3/4" (2 cm) high, extensive colonies to 65' (20 m) across in spots. Divides to form colony of white to pink, lavender to red bodies, white knobs at tips of tentacles. On current-swept rocks, intertidal to at least 150' (45 m).

Sea Anemones

▼ GIANT (Frilled) PLUMOSE ANEMONE

Metridium farcimen (=M. giganteum)
To 3' (1 m) high, 12" (30 cm) diameter.
Smooth column, lobed oral disc with
more than 200 slender, translucent tentacles. White, brown or tan to orange.
Dense aggregations on floats and rocks,
intertidal to 1,000' (300 m) deep.

◄ PLUMOSE ANEMONE

Metridium senile
To 4" (10 cm) high,
2" (5 cm) diameter.
Oral disc not lobed;
fewer than 100
slender tentacles
grow from it.
White, tan to
brown, orange.
Dense aggregations
on rocks and floats,
intertidal to 1,000'
(300 m) deep.

▼ PAINTED ANEMONE

Urticina crassicornis
To 5" (12.5 cm) high, 3" (7.5 cm)
diameter. Column variable in colour,
with green, red and yellow patches.
Rings of short, thick, coloured or
banded tentacles, about 100 in all. On
rocks, intertidal and shallow subtidal.

▼ STUBBY BURIED ANEMONE

Urticina coriacea
To 6" (15 cm) high and wide. Red column, usually partially buried in
sand–mud. Green to olive disc has short,
blunt, banded tentacles of green, pink,
red or blue. Intertidal to 50' (15 m) deep.

◄ FISH-EATING ANEMONE

Urticina piscivora
To 10" (25 cm) high, 8" (20 cm)
diameter. Tall, smooth red-maroon
column. Long, slender white, red or
pink tentacles. On rocks on open
coast, 20–100' (6–30 m) deep.

WHITE-SPOTTED ANEMONE ▸
Urticina lofotensis
To 6" (15 cm) high and wide. Squat
scarlet column with vertical rows of
white tubercles (projections). Long
yellow tentacles with pink tips. On
exposed rocky coasts, intertidal to 50'
(15 m) deep.

▲ SAND ANEMONE
Urticina columbiana
To 10" (25 cm) high, 14" (35 cm)
diameter. Column, partially buried in
sand, has rough tubercles (projections).
Long, slender, white to pink tentacles.
In sand–mud–shell, subtidal to 150'
(45 m) or deeper.

▼ GIANT GREEN ANEMONE
Anthopleura xanthogrammica
To 12" (30 cm) high, 10" (25 cm)
diameter. Column green to olive, tentacles and oral disc uniform green from
algae living symbiotically in the tissues.
On open coast, intertidal, tidepools
and shallow subtidal.

▼ AGGREGATE GREEN ANEMONE
Anthopleura elegantissima
To 6" (15 cm) high, 3" (7.5 cm) diameter. Budding colonies. Green beaded
column, pale green tentacles with pink
tips, shown here open and closed
(inset photo). On rocks or in current,
intertidal and shallow subtidal.

▼ BURIED MOONGLOW ANEMONE *Anthopleura artemisia*
To 10" (25 cm) high, 4" (10 cm) diame-
ter. Column mostly buried. Long, slender
tentacles, pink, orange or luminous
green-grey, with white bands. In sand,
intertidal to 35' (10 m) deep.

▲ BROODING ANEMONE
Epiactis prolifera
To 4" (10 cm) high, 2" (5 cm) diameter.
Low, squat. Vertical white lines on
column and radiating lines on disk. Colour
varies from pink to green, brown and
orange. Young anemones exit mouth; up to
30 young are fixed on the column.
Intertidal to 30' (9 m) deep.

▼ SNAKELOCK ANEMONE
Cribrinopsis fernaldi
Column to 8" (20 cm) high, with longitudinal rows of tubercles, 6" (15 cm) diameter.
Long, slender, drooping tentacles with distinctive raised zigzag lines. White to pink to
red. Candystripe and broken back shrimp
(p. 44) live under canopy of tentacles. On
rocks, subtidal to 1,000' (300 m) deep.

▼ SWIMMING ANEMONE
Stomphia didemon
To 4" (10 cm) high, 5" (12.5 cm)
diameter. Cream to orange, sometimes mottled column with
orange, white or banded tentacles.
Swims to escape the leather star
(p. 49). On rocks, subtidal to 65'
(20 m) deep.

▼ TUBE-DWELLING ANEMONE
Pachycerianthus fimbriatus
To 14" (35 cm) long, crown to 8"
(20 cm) diameter. Secretes mucus-
like tube to 3' (1 m) long in mud.
2 sets of golden brown to purple
or black tentacles; short inner
circle of tentacles over mouth.
Eaten by nudibranchs. Intertidal
to 100' (30 m).

Hydroids, Jellyfish & Comb Jellies

Phylum Cnidaria
Phylum Ctenophora

Hydroids

The hydroid is a small animal, which consists of a stalk crowned with a ring of tentacles. Individuals form colonies that resemble bushy plants. A variety of nudibranchs (sea slugs) feed on hydroids.

▼ PINK MOUTH HYDROID
Ectopleura marina
To 3" (7.5 cm) high. Solitary. Orange-pink polyp on slender stalk. On rocks and floats, intertidal to 50' (15 m) deep.

▲ PINK HEART HYDROID
Ectopleura crocea
To 5" (12.5 cm) high, colonies more than 12" (30 cm) across. Tangles of straw-like stems; pink and red polyps with grape-like clusters of reproductive organs. On rocks, intertidal to 50' (15 m).

▲ OSTRICH PLUME HYDROID
Aglaophenia struthionides
To 5" (12.5 cm) high. Polyps are on one side of each feather-like branch (visible only by close inspection, not in photo). Elongated yellow eggs on plumes. On rocks, intertidal to 525' (157 m) deep.

SEA FIR ▶
Abietinaria sp.
To 6" (15 cm) high. Fern-like stem and branches. Polyps on both sides of branches. On rocks, intertidal to 60' (20 m).

SNAIL FUR ▶
Hydractinia milleri
To 1/8" (3 mm) high, mats to 2" (5 cm) diameter. Pink, fuzzy mass, joined at the base in a mat that unites the colony. Grows on shells inhabited by hermit crabs (p. 43–44), shells of crabs and occasionally rocks. Stinging capsules may deter predators. Intertidal to 80' (24 m).

◀ **ORANGE HYDROID**
Garveia annulata
To 6" (15 cm) high. Clusters to 12" (30 cm) across of bright orange stems and polyps. On rocks, kelp and sponges, intertidal to 400' (120 m) deep.

Jellyfish

MOON JELLY ▶
Aurelia labiata
To 3" (7.5 cm) high, 8" (20 cm) diameter. 4 horseshoe gonads visible in clear, grey- to blue-tinged bell. Bell scalloped into 8 pairs of lobes. Short marginal tentacles. In coastal waters, bays and harbours.

▼ SEA BLUBBER
Cyanea capillata
Typically to 20" (50 cm); northern specimens to 7' (2 m) diameter. Trailing tentacles to 30' (9 m). 8 pairs of lobes around edge of bell. Red-brown to yellow, rose to white body. Tentacles cause stinging and burning. In coastal waters, bays and harbours.

▼ SAIL JELLYFISH *Velella velella*
To 3" (7.5 cm) long. Jellyfish-like hydroid colony. Dark blue-purple, with an upright triangular sail. Floats on the surface, often blown onto beaches.

▾ CLINGING JELLYFISH
Gonionemus vertens
To 1¼" (6 mm) diameter. Jellyfish-like hydroid colony Transparent bell contains cross-shaped gonads coloured red or orange, to brown or violet. Long tentacles have adhesive pads. Attached to kelp and eelgrass in intertidal and shallow subtidal.

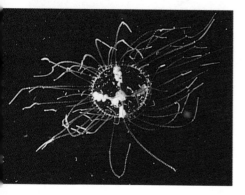

Comb jellies
Phylum Ctenophora
These jellyfish-like animals have sticky cells on their tentacles, rather than stinging cells, which they use to capture food.

▾ CAT'S EYE COMB JELLY
Pleurobrachia bachei
To ½" (1 cm) high, 2 trailing tentacles 6" (15 cm) or longer. Round to egg-shaped body with combs (rows of cilia) in a rainbow of colours. In shallow waters, spring to autumn. Often washed ashore (inset photo).

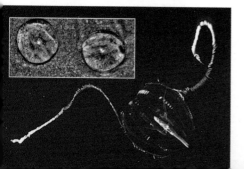

Sponges
Phylum Porifera

Sponges are small animals that feed by filtering water through pores and chambers (*Porifera* means "hole bearers"). Individuals grow in colonies that range in form from thin mats and crusts to erect tube-like, vase-like or branching masses. The support structure may be calcareous (containing calcium carbonate), or made of siliceous spicules (pointed glass protrusions) or spongin, a tough protein network. Sponges are common on rocks, floats and pilings; intertidal to great depths. They are eaten by nudibranchs (sea slugs), some snails and sea stars.

▾ TUBE SPONGE
Leucosolenia nautilia
Tubes to ⅛" (3 mm) diameter, forming loose branching colonies to 2–6" (5–15 cm) diameter. Calcareous. On rocks and floats, intertidal and shallow subtidal.

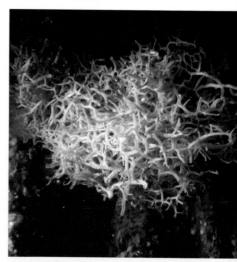

▲ PURPLE SPONGE
Haliclona permollis
Encrusting to 1⁵/₈" high, 3' (1 m) diameter. Raised volcano-like oscula (pores). Pink or lavender to purple. Often eaten by leopard dorid nudibranch (p. 18). On rocks, intertidal.

▲ BREAD CRUMB SPONGE
Halichondria panicea (spp.)
Encrusting to 2" (5 cm) high, 12" (30 cm) or more diameter. Prominent low, volcano-like oscula (pores). Yellow to green. When broken, smells like exploded gunpowder. On rocks and floats, intertidal and shallow subtidal.

▼ VELVETY RED SPONGE
Ophlitaspongia pennata
Thin crust to 1/4" (6 mm) thick, to 3' (1 m) diameter. Smooth patches. Coral red, red-brown to mustard colour. Often found with red nudibranch (p. 19) feeding and laying a ribbon of eggs. On rocks, intertidal to 295' (90 m) deep.

▼ YELLOW BORING SPONGE
Cliona celata var. californiana
Encrusting as yellow spots, patches or masses on shells, protruding from holes to 1/8" (3 mm) diameter. Bores into shells, particularly rock scallop (p. 28) and barnacle (p. 46); sometimes on rocks. Low intertidal to 400' (120 m) deep.

◀ ROUGH ENCRUSTING
(Scallop) SPONGE *Myxilla incrustans*
Encrusting to 3/8" (9 mm) thick on shell of spiny pink scallop (p. 29). Gold to light brown, with lumpy oscula (pores). Often eaten by nudibranchs. On swimming scallops, 3–500' (1–150 m) deep.

SMOOTH ENCRUSTING (Scallop) SPONGE ▶
Mycale adhaerans
Encrusting to 3/8" (9 mm) thick on shell of spiny pink scallop (p. 29). Yellow-brown to violet. Smoother and smaller oscula (pores) than rough encrusting sponge. On swimming scallops, 3–500' (1–150 m) deep.

◀ HERMIT CRAB SPONGE
Suberites suberea
Encrusting lumps to 3" (7.5 cm) high and wide. Settles on and dissolves shells inhabited by hermit crabs. Grey, brown to dark orange. Hermit crabs grow within the growing sponge and do not need to fight for larger shells. Low intertidal to 120' (36 m) deep.

◀ WESTERN NIPPLE SPONGE *Polymastia pacifica*
Mat to 1/4" (6 mm) thick, 12" (30 cm) diameter. Many raised nipple-like oscula (pores) to 3/8" (9 mm) high. Cream-yellow. On rocks, intertidal to 600' (180 m) deep.

▼ CLOUD SPONGE
Aphrocallistes vastus
Large, erect, to 6 1/2' (2 m) high, branching growths to 10' (3 m) diameter. Siliceous with 6-rayed spicules (pointed projections). On rocks in inlets, 80' (24 m) and deeper.

▼ CHIMNEY (Boot) SPONGE
Rhabdocalyptus dawsoni
Large tube to 5' (1.5 m) high, 3' (1 m) diameter. Siliceous, with 6-rayed spicules (pointed projections). Thin-lipped oscula (pores). Sediment is trapped in body bristles. Hangs on rock walls or stands on rocks, 40' (12 m) and deeper.

▼ TENNIS BALL SPONGE
Craniella villosa
Globular, to 6" (15 cm) diameter. Grey exterior with a ridge and holes on top; white to yellow interior. On rocks, intertidal to 65' (20 m) deep.

▼ ORANGE PUFFBALL SPONGE
Tethya californiana (=T. aurantia)
Globular, to 6" (15 cm) diameter. Rough surface with many ostia (small pores). Orange or yellow to green in colour. On rocks, often in muddy areas, 20' (6 m) and deeper.

Worms

Phylum Annelida, Phylum Nemertea, Phylum Platyhelminthes

Segmented Worms
Phylum Annelida
The bodies of these worms are divided into obvious segments by encircling grooves. They may have bristles or paddle-like appendages. A segmented worm may be free-moving, or burrowing, or fixed in a tube with only the head visible, modified as a plume.

▼ NORTHERN FEATHER DUSTER WORM
Eudistylia vancouveri
Tube to 2' (60 cm) high, 1/2" (1 cm) diameter; worm to 6" (15 cm) diameter, plume to 2" (5 cm) across. Distinctive banded green and maroon plumes protrude from long, light grey or brown parchment-like tubes. On rocks and floats, intertidal to 65' (20 m).

▼ CALCAREOUS TUBE WORM
Serpula vermicularis
Tube to 4" (10 cm) long, 1/4" (6 mm) diameter; worm to 4" (10 cm) long; plume to 3/4" (2 cm) diameter. White, rambling, limy tubes. Tentacles red, sometimes banded with white. Conical stoppers close off tube as worm withdraws. Tubes attached to rocks, pilings or floats, often on underside, intertidal to at least 330' (100 m).

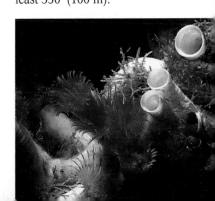

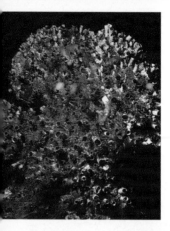

◀ FRINGED TUBE WORM
Dodecaceria fewkesi
Tubes to 1⁵/8" (4 cm) long, ¹/8" (3 mm) wide, in clumps to 3' (1 m) diameter. Short, hard, limy tube. Dark brown or green to black body with 11 pairs of dark filaments growing from head. On rocks, intertidal to 65' (20 m).

PACIFIC LUGWORM and CASTINGS
Abarenicola pacifica ▼
To 6" (15 cm) long. A burrowing worm found near coiled pile of castings. Green to red body, red gills when wet. On sand–mud beaches, high intertidal.

▲ MUSSEL (Pile) WORM
Nereis vexillosa
To 12" (30 cm) long. Many large paddle-like feet. Dark, iridescent green, blue and grey. Everts pincer-like jaws to feed. Free-moving in mussel beds or mud–gravel of clam beds, or burrowed in sand–mud–gravel, intertidal and shallow subtidal.

▼ SCALE WORM
Halsydna brevisetosa
To 2³/8" (6 cm) long. Slender, brown-grey body with 18 pairs of black-spotted scales along back. Free-living on floats, in mussel beds or under rocks, intertidal to 1,790' (540 m).

Ribbon Worms
Phylum Nemertea
These worms have long, thin, somewhat flattened bodies that are not segmented. They are found under rocks and in barnacle clumps, mussel beds and kelp holdfasts. The ribbon worm attacks its prey with a proboscis, a long feeding apparatus that shoots out from the head.

GREEN AND YELLOW RIBBON WORM
Emplectonema gracile ▼
To 4" (10 cm) long and ¹/16" (2 mm) wide. Dark green on top, yellowish green below. Under rocks, in barnacle clusters, in mussel beds, intertidal.

▼ ORANGE RIBBON WORM

Tubulanus polymorphus
To 10" (25 cm) long, 3/16" (5 mm) wide. Thin, often coiled body with broad, rounded head. Bright orange. Under rocks, intertidal to 165' (50 m) deep.

Flatworms

Phylum Platyhelminthes
The flatworms have flattened oval bodies. They are free-moving, and are usually seen under rocks, in mussel beds and in tunicates (see p. 69).

▼ GIANT FLATWORM

Kaburakia excelsa
To 4" (10 cm) long, 2 3/4" (5.6 cm) wide, 1/8" (3 mm) thick. Firm oval body. 2 short tentacles with eye spots. Orange to brown, spotted. Under rocks and in mussel beds, intertidal.

Other Small Marine Animals

Moss Animals (Bryozoans), Sea Squirts & Tunicates

Moss Animals (Bryozoans)

Phylum Bryozoa
These tiny animals live in colonies that resemble moss. Tiny individuals are cased in box-like or tube-like units of limy, calcareous or other stiff material. A crown of fringed tentacles protrudes from each pore. The animals often divide to reproduce.

▼ STAGHORN BRYOZOAN

Heteropora magna
Colony to 2" (5 cm) high, to 6" (15 cm) diameter. Greenish branches, not joined, with rounded yellow tips. On rocks, subtidal to 90' (27 m) deep.

KELP LACY BRYOZOAN
(Lacy Crust) ▶
Membranipora membrancea
Thin, lacy crusts to 3" (7.5 cm) diameter. Silver patches of small intersecting "boxes." On kelp, floats and rocks, shallow subtidal.

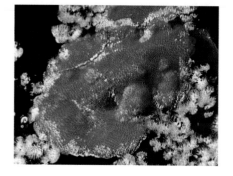

◀ ORANGE CRUST BRYOZOAN
Schizoporella unicornis
Thin crust to 2" (5 cm) diameter. Orange, brown or golden with fine pattern of pores. On rocks, shells, floats and kelp, intertidal to 200' (60 m) deep.

▼ SPIRAL BRYOZOAN
Bugula californica
One or more spirals to 2³/4" (7 cm) high. Branches grow in whorls, whitish-tan to orange. On rocks and shells, shallow subtidal to 1,320' (400 m) deep.

▲ LACY BRYOZOAN
Phidolorphora labiata
To 2¹/2" (5 cm) high, 8¹/2" (21 cm) diameter. Stiff, brittle, ruffled formation, salmon pink to orange or white. Shown here with purple-ring topsnail (p. 33). On rocks, intertidal to 660' (200 m) deep.

SCULPTURED BRYOZOAN ▶
Hippodiplosia insculpta
To 4" (10 cm) high, 4" (10 cm) diameter. Layered frills with double-fluted branches, yellow-tan to orange. On rocks, subtidal to 770' (230 m) deep.

STICK BRYOZOAN ▶
Microporina borealis
To 4" (10 cm) high, 4" (10 cm) diameter. Short, jointed segments, elliptical in cross-section. Yellow-cream to tan. On rocks, shallow subtidal to 1,320' (400 m) deep.

▲ WHITE BRANCHING BRYOZOAN
Diaperoecia californica
Masses to 1" (2.5 cm) high and 10" (25 cm) across in spots. White to dark yellow, flattened branches. On rocks, shells and giant kelps, subtidal to 600' (180 m) deep.

▼ LEATHER BRYOZOAN
Flustrellidra corniculata
To 4" (10 cm) high, 2" (5 cm) across in spots. Flattened leathery branches, tan with short brown spines along the edges. On rocks and shells, intertidal to 245' (73 m) deep.

Sea Squirts, Tunicates (Compound Ascidians)
Phylum Urochordata
These colourful, jelly-like animals resemble sponges. Each individual has 2 siphons to pump water through the body. Colonies often carpet floats and the seafloor. Individuals may be solitary in form (sea squirts), or occur in aggregations or compound ascidian colonies (tunicates, so-called because individuals are embedded in a common skin-like tunic).

▼ STALKED HAIRY SEA SQUIRT *Boltenia villosa*
To 1 5/8" (4 cm) high, 1 1/4" (3 cm) wide. Solitary. Stalk with red-orange, tan to brown tunic, covered with hairs or spines. Low intertidal to 330' (99 m) deep.

▲ STALKED SEA SQUIRT
Styela montereyensis
To 10" (25 cm) high. Solitary. Long, thin stalk, grooved, with 2 siphons at the tip, one straight and one bent over. Orange-red to brown. In currents, on rocks, intertidal to 100' (30 m) deep.

▼ SEA PEACH
Halocynthia aurantium
To 6" (15 cm) high. Solitary. Smooth and barrel-shaped with large projecting siphons. Orange-red. On rocks, subtidal to 330' (99 m) deep.

▼ SHINY ORANGE SEA SQUIRT
Cnemidocarpa finmarkiensis
To 3" (7.5 cm) high, 2" (5 cm) diameter. Solitary. Smooth, squat pearly orange-red tunic. Short projecting siphons. On rocks, intertidal to 165' (50 m) deep.

▼ WRINKLED SEA SQUIRT
Pyura haustor
To 3" (7.5 cm) high, 3" (7.5 cm) diameter. Solitary. Distinctive long, slender red-pink siphons protrude from warty base. In clusters, on rocks, intertidal to 660' (200 m) deep.

◀ GLASSY SEA SQUIRT
Ascidia paratropa
To 6" (15 cm) high. Solitary. Clear cylindrical tunic with obvious fleshy spines, prominent siphons. On rocks, in current areas, intertidal to 265' (80 m) deep.

▲ SPINY SEA SQUIRT
Halocynthia igaboja
To 4" (10 cm) high, 4" (10 cm) diameter. Globular, spiny body, often grey-black with silt. Reddish siphons close to form a cross shape. On rocks, intertidal to 540' (162 m) deep.

LIGHT BULB ASCIDIAN
Clavelina huntsmani ▼
To 2" (5 cm) high, clusters to 20" (50 cm) across. Colonial. Transparent tubes, each with 2 orange-pink "filaments." On rocks, subtidal to 100' (30 m) deep.

▲ ORANGE SOCIAL ASCIDIANS *Metandrocarpa taylori*
To 1/4" (6 mm) high. Clustered individuals joined by a slender stolon (stem-like structure) or thin tunic sheet. On rocks, in currents, intertidal to 65' (20 m) deep.

▼ LOBED ASCIDIAN *Cystodytes lobatus*
To 1 1/2" (3.8 cm) thick, patches to 10" (25 cm) or more diameter. Encrusting colony with irregular ridges and lobes. Grey or purple-pink. On exposed coasts, on rocks, intertidal to 660' (200 m) deep.

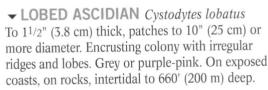

▼ SEA PORK
Aplidium californicum
To 1³/₄" (4.4 cm) thick, 12" (30 cm) across. Encrusting sheets. Yellow, grey, opalescent white or transparent colonies. On rocks, in current or wave-exposed areas, intertidal to 280' (85 m) deep.

▼ MUSHROOM ASCIDIAN
Distaplia occidentalis
To 1¹/₂" (3.8 cm) high, 4" (10 cm) across. Colonies, mushroom-shaped to flattened, rounded. Variable colours from white to grey, yellow, pink, red, or purple-brown. On rocks, in currents or surge, intertidal to 50' (15 m) deep.

Seaweeds & Seagrasses

There may be as many as 700 species of seaweeds, microscopic algae and sea grasses along the Pacific Coast from Alaska to California.

Green Seaweeds
Phylum Chlorophyta
These seaweeds, typically grass green or olive green, grow in shallow waters. Most species are less than 12" (30 cm) long, including filaments, blades, cylinders, spongy mats and spheres.

▼ SEA LETTUCE *Ulva* spp.
To 7" (17.5 cm) long and wide. Thin blades, often with ruffled or incised edges. Small, distinct stipe (stem). Bright green. Common, but difficult to identify positively in habitat. Along protected shores, mid- to low intertidal.

▼ SEA HAIR (Tubeweed)
Enteromorpha spp.
To 8" (20 cm) long, to ¹/₄" (6 mm) diameter. Stringy mats, yellow-green to dark green. Difficult to identify positively in habitat. Free-floating in tidepools, attached to rocks in high to mid-intertidal.

▼ SEA STAGHORN
Codium fragile
To 16" (39 cm) high. Sponge-like, branching growths. Dark green. In tidepools and among rocks, mid- to low intertidal.

▼ GREEN SPONGY CUSHION
Codium setchellii
To $3/4$" (2 cm) thick and 10" (25 cm) diameter. Sponge-like, shiny dark green patches. Low intertidal.

▼ GREEN TUFT *Cladophora* sp.
To 2" (5 cm) high and 12" (30 cm) diameter. Bright green filamentous tufts. On rocks along exposed to protected shores, mid- to low intertidal.

Brown Seaweeds
Phylum Phaeophyta
These are the largest and most visible seaweeds on the coast. They range in colour from olive green to dark brown to almost black. The brown seaweeds occur as crusts, filaments, globular, flat-bladed, branched-bladed, feather-like and ribbed forms.

▼ ROCKWEED
Fucus gardneri
Flattened branches to 20" (50 cm) long. Midrib on olive green to yellow-brown branches; swollen terminal ends. On rocks, mid- to low intertidal.

▼ LITTLE ROCKWEED
Pelvetiopsis limitata
To $3^1/4$" (8 cm) tall. Flattened stems without midribs; swollen terminal ends. Light tan to olive. On rocks, high intertidal.

▲ SEA CAULIFLOWER
Leathesia difformis
To 1" (2.5 cm) tall, 5" (12.5 cm) diameter. Convoluted and globular.
Yellowish brown to golden. Attached to rocks, mid-intertidal.

▼ BULL KELP
Nereocystis luetkeana
Stalk to 65' (20 m) long. Float (reproductive part) to 5" (12.5 cm) diameter.
Broad, flat blades to 10' (3 m) long, 8" (20 cm) wide. Olive to dark brown.
Attached by holdfast to rocks, forming kelp beds on protected to exposed shores, lowest intertidal to 65' (20 m) deep.

▼ SMALL PERENNIAL KELP (Northern Giant Kelp)
Macrocystis integrifolia
To 99' (30 m) long. Flattened holdfast (a feature that distinguishes this species from a similar one). Numerous branches, slit blades and pear-shaped floats (reproductive parts) form extensive canopies. Olive to dark brown. In sheltered waters along the open coast, lowest intertidal to 33' (10 m) deep.

▼ WIREWEED (Sargassum)
Sargassum muticum
To 10' (3 m) tall. Short stock, branching repeatedly, spherical floats (reproductive parts). Introduced from Japan. Attached to rocks or shells, low intertidal to 16' (5 m) deep.

▲ SEA PALM
Postelsia palmaeformis
To 2' (60 cm) tall. Stubby holdfast. Long, flexible stalk with numerous drooping blades to 10" (25 cm) long. Greenish to olive-brown. On surf-exposed rocks, mid- to low intertidal.

▼ FEATHER BOA
Egregia menziesii
To 65' (19.5 m) long. Strap-like stem, densely covered with blades and elongated floats to 2" (5 cm) long. Olive to dark brown. On exposed coasts, intertidal to 65' (320 m) deep.

Red Seaweeds
Phylum Rhodophyta
The red seaweeds live at greater depths than others. Colours range from shades of red and brown to purple and black. Species occur in encrusting patches, in a filamentous form, or in large, conspicuous blades that may be smooth or ribbed.

▼ PURPLE LAVER
Porphyra perforata
To 12" (30 cm) long and wide. Tiny, disc-shaped holdfast. Thin, broad, delicate, lobed or ruffled blade. Iridescent purple to purple-green. On rocks, mussels and other algae along protected and exposed shores, upper to mid-intertidal.

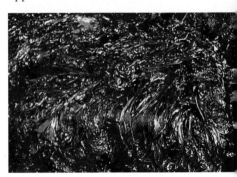

▼ TURKISH TOWEL
Chondracanthuds exasperatus
To 16" (39 cm) long. Broad, thick, unbranched blades, bearing stiff projections. Brick red to shades of purple, iridescent when wet. The most common of several similar species. On intertidal rocks and subtidal to 65' (20 m).

▲ NAIL BRUSH
Endocladia muricata
To 3" (7.5 cm) tall. Dense, stiff, bushy clumps of cylindrical branches. Pinkish or dark red to black-brown. On rocks and mussels along exposed shores, upper to mid-intertidal.

▲ BLACK PINE
Neorhodomela larix
To 12" (30 cm) long. Wiry branches with small clusters of ringlets. Dark brown-black. Coarse mats on sandy, rocky reefs, upper to low intertidal.

▼ PINK ROCK CRUST
Lithothamnion spp. and others
To 1/8" (3 mm) thick, often round to 4" (10 cm) diameter. Smooth or covered with bumps. Pink. Common, but difficult to identify positively without microscopic examination. On rocks and shells, intertidal to 33' (10 m).

▲ SEA SAC
Halosaccion glandiforme
To 6" (15 cm) long, 3/4" (2 cm) wide. Groups of finger-like sacs. Bright purple-red to pale yellow. On rocks, in a band along exposed and transition shores, mid-intertidal.

▼ BRANCHING CORALLINE ALGAE *Corallina, Calliarthron* and *Bosiella* spp.
To at least 6" (15 cm) tall. Flattened branches with jointed segments. Common, but difficult to identify positively without microscopic examination. In tidepools, lower intertidal, shallow subtidal.

Seagrasses
Phylum Anthophyta
These rooted aquatic seed plants form important, productive shoreline habitats for many fishes and marine animals. They are not true grasses but flowering plants related to lilies.

▼ DWARF EELGRASS
Zostera japonica
Thin blades to 8" (20 cm) long, less than 1/8" (6 mm) wide. Dark green. Introduced from Japan. Along wave-protected shores, intertidal, higher on beach than eelgrass.

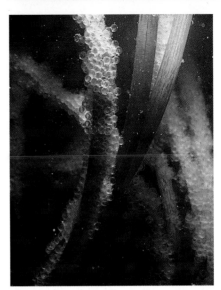

▲ EELGRASS
Zostera marina
Flat blades to 4' (1.2 m) long, 1/4" (6 mm) wide. Dull green. Rooted in sand and mud in wave-protected areas, low intertidal to shallow subtidal, at least 33' (10 m) deep. Shown here coated with herring spawn.

▼ (Scouler's) SURFGRASS
Phyllospadix scouleri
Flat, narrow blades to 3' (90 cm) long, to 1/8" (6 mm) wide. Bright emerald green. Attached to intertidal rocks on surf-exposed shores.

Semi-Marine Plants
Phylum Anthophyta

▼ SEA ASPARAGUS
(Pickleweed) *Salicornia virginica*
Spreading, branching mats to 10" (25 cm) tall. Along protected shores, tide flats and salt-water marshes, high intertidal.